A WEEK BY WEEK GUIDE TO YOUR BABY'S
FIRST YEAR

MAGGIE JONES

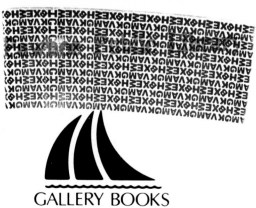

GALLERY BOOKS

An Imprint of W. H. Smith Publishers Inc.

112 Madison Avenue
New York City 10016

Contents

Weeks 27-39

6–9 months

Weeks 40-52

9–12 months

First published in 1988 by
Conran Octopus Limited
37 Shelton Street
London WC2H 9HN

This edition published
in 1989 by Gallery Books,
an imprint of W.H. Smith Publishers Inc.,
112 Madison Avenue, New York, New York 10016,
in association with Conran Octopus Limited

ISBN 0-8317-3228-8
Typeset by Tradespools Limited
Printed and bound in Hong Kong

Introduction

This book is a week-by-week guide to the first year of your baby's life. It aims to describe in detail the various stages of a baby's progress, to give practical advice and to help parents cope with, and enjoy, their baby at every age.

Wherever possible, the information you will need appears on the page most appropriate to the age and stage your baby is at. However, this is not always feasible. First of all, the huge amount of information relevant to the early days has had to be spread over the first few weeks, though you may well wish to read it all at once. Secondly, babies develop at very different rates. Some will be crawling at six months and others not until ten months or later; some babies will be sitting up at five months and others not until nine months. Some babies are physically very active and mobile, others concentrate more on how to use their hands or on learning to speak early. So don't be worried if your baby isn't doing what it says on that particular week; it doesn't mean he or she is in any way abnormal!

Cross-references are included wherever necessary, and at the back of the book is a full index, to help you look up information on a particular topic if you do not find it in the week that seems appropriate to your baby.

At regular intervals in the book you will find information on how and what to feed your baby. This follows the recommendations now made by pediatricians on what is best for a growing baby. Of course, you can vary this if you have good cause – always discuss your reasons for weaning or any change in diet with your doctor. For example, if your baby is doing well on breast-milk or formula alone, there is no need to wean him or her as fast as this book suggests, although you should be adding some solids to your child's diet after six months or so.

You might well like to use the space on the left-hand pages to write down appointments and reminders of things you have to do, as well as to keep a note of your feelings. You can also use it to keep a record of your baby's progress, recording the day he first smiles or learns to crawl or when he takes his first dramatic steps. The book is also meant to give you tips and information which will help remind you of when your baby needs his first vaccinations, for example, or when you should schedule a postpartum checkup for yourself. Each week, fill in the Month and Dates at the top of the page for that particular week – for example, November 24th–30th – so that you can use the guide for specific appointments when you need to.

This book is aimed not only at mothers but at both the baby's parents. Modern fathers have a wonderful opportunity to learn to share in the joys and the hard work of parenthood. If you are a working mother, it is even more important that your partner shares in household tasks and helps care for the baby as well as providing another source of security and fun.

Above all, we believe that looking after your baby should be fun as well as, inevitably, being hard work and a great responsibility. So we have included ideas for games and activities which you can enjoy with the baby at various different stages in his or her development.

The baby is referred to as "he" or "she" in alternate chapters throughout the book to reflect the fact that the text applies equally to male and female children. The term "partner" has been chosen to cover the baby's father, no matter what his status.

There is a list of useful addresses at the end of the book. Refer to the groups or associations if you would like more information about a particular aspect whose detailed coverage is beyond the scope of this book.

A note about the author
Maggie Jones's second child had just celebrated his first birthday when she started to write this book, so all the problems and rewards of a baby's first precious year were fresh in her mind as she wrote. Like many babies, hers did not behave as most of the baby books assume they should, and she frequently found herself wondering what on earth to try next!

She intends in this book to share some of the tips and solutions to their problems that she and other mothers found, as well as providing practical information. She hopes also to convey some of the pleasures, as well as the hard work, of bringing up a baby.

Maggie Jones is 34 years old and has written several books, mostly on aspects of pregnancy and childcare.

Week 1

MON

TUES

WED

THURS

FRI

SAT

SUN

Notes

HANDLING YOUR BABY

When you pick your new baby up, always take care to support his head. Babies like to be held closely and handled confidently – this makes them feel secure. Hold your baby against your shoulder, supporting his head, or cradled in your arm so that he can look up at your face. Baby carriers or slings give this closeness and sense of security while enabling you to get other things done (see Week 3).

Most new mothers and fathers are afraid of dropping their babies or of harming them by mistake, and may also be nervous of changing and bathing them. Remember that a baby will sense your nervousness and that it is therefore important to handle him firmly but gently; talk to your baby to reassure him too.

When you pick your baby up, slip your hand under his head to prevent it from flopping backwards, and use the other hand to support the rest of his body.

Many babies like to be carried with their head resting on your shoulder. Use one hand to support his bottom and the other to prevent his head from flopping back away from your shoulder.

DON'T FORGET You should schedule your baby's first checkup with the pediatrician or family doctor. The first "well-baby" checkup is routinely done two to four weeks after the baby's birth.

Feeding your baby

Most pediatricians will be very helpful in resolving any initial problems, either at the hospital or once you get home. The La Leche League also has breast-feeding counselors who will help (see Week 7).

Some women experience more difficulties than others in breast-feeding and some just do not enjoy it. Don't waste energy feeling guilty if you decide to bottle-feed: most babies will thrive on formula milk. Remember that what your baby needs most is love and attention, so make sure he is getting plenty of both.

Putting your baby to the breast
The baby's mouth should be wide open and should cover the areola, the dark-colored area around the nipple, not just the nipple itself. If you touch your baby's cheek with your breast he will automatically turn his head towards the breast and open his mouth, ready to feed.

The main concern of every new mother is how to feed her baby. Most modern mothers will know that breast-feeding is best for their babies. Not only is a mother's milk perfectly adapted for the baby's needs, it also contains antibodies to infections which will protect him in the early weeks.

If you want to breast-feed it is important that the baby is put to the breast as soon as possible after delivery. For the first few days the breasts produce a yellowish substance called colostrum, which is rich in protein and antibodies. The mature milk generally comes in on the third or fourth day after the birth, and usually looks rather watery.

Some mothers find that their nipples get rather sore to begin with and their breasts may be painful when the milk first comes in. Some babies are slow to get the idea of breast-feeding and may take some time to get "latched on" properly. Unless he is correctly latched on, your nipples will get sore and the baby will not get enough milk. Remember to start each feeding on a different breast.

It is very important that all equipment used for bottle-feeding (whether you are giving formula or expressed milk or cooled, boiled water) is thoroughly washed and sterilized. If you don't feel confident about whether you are doing this properly, ask your pediatrician or physician for advice.

Breast-fed babies may feed very often, sometimes as much as every two hours and some need ten to twelve feedings in 24 hours. Many mothers worry that their breastmilk is inadequate and consider whether they should supplement with formula. The truth is that the more frequently the baby nurses, the more milk the breasts will produce. As the baby gets bigger he will take more milk at each feeding and need to nurse less often.

Don't think that hunger is always the reason why your baby is crying. Many babies cry because they miss the movement and warmth of the womb, or because they are tired, uncomfortable or just bored. If you really want to breast-feed, have confidence that you will produce enough milk and make sure you get enough rest and eat well.

Week 2

Month: Dates:

MON

TUES

WED

THURS

FRI

SAT

SUN

Notes

At two to four weeks, the baby usually has the first of her routine "well-baby" checkups (see p. 19). At this visit, your pediatrician or family doctor will do a thorough, "get acquainted" examination to see that your baby is developing properly. This will be a relatively long appointment. Your baby will be examined to see that she has normal reflexes and is putting on weight well. The doctor will listen to her chest and will check that she does not have any abnormality. The doctor will also do a simple test for dislocated hips, by pushing up her legs and rotating them, and he will also check for undescended testicles if you have a boy.

The doctor will ensure that the cord has healed properly and will ask you if you have any worries about your baby. This will be a perfect opportunity for you to discuss any concerns you may have regarding feeding, sleep, development, etc.

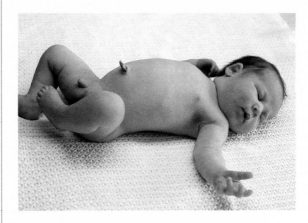

The umbilical cord is cut quite short and securely clamped. It is initially translucent and jelly-like but soon begins to dry and shrivel. It usually drops off within ten days or so, but it may go black, bleed a little and look very ugly in the meantime.

◼ **DON'T FORGET** Take the time to write down all emergency phone numbers – doctor, ambulance, police, fire department, poison control center – and keep them posted near your phone.

Getting home from hospital

The first few days after your baby is born will probably be spent in the hospital, and you will look forward to returning home and starting your new life with the baby in familiar surroundings. However, for many mothers the idea of coping with the baby on their own can seem quite frightening – there may be no one at hand to advise you what to do if she acts in an unexpected way. Also, most babies sleep a lot in the hospital during the few days after the birth, and going home may coincide with her having wakeful periods or crying and fretting a lot. This can make the new mother feel she is doing something wrong.

Remember that your doctor and his assistants are there to help you if you have any questions about your baby's health or questions regarding your baby's general care. If you are calling because you believe your

Relaxing together
In the first few days, try to get friends, relatives or your partner to cope with all the necessary chores in the house while you concentrate on yourself and the baby, and on getting the rest you need.

baby may be ill, it can help to make a list of significant points before you call: Does your baby have a temperature? Has there been a change in the amount she has eaten recently? Is she irritable or lethargic? Is she pale or flushed? How frequent or infrequent have her bowel movements been?

Most newborn babies will have fretful periods in the day or evening; if you are breast-feeding, do not automatically assume that she is crying because she is still hungry. A newborn baby will root around for the breast even when not hungry because the breast is her main source of comfort. If your baby is crying for no apparent reason, and has been fed recently, try walking around with her in a carrier or sling or held close to the body, or swaddle her and rock her in a carriage or cradle. A lullaby tape or a musical toy may have a soothing effect. Some babies are just unusually wakeful.

'Postnatal blues'
Many mothers feel weepy and emotional in the first days or weeks after the birth. Some women find they have a weepy period around the third or fourth day, when their milk comes in; this can be partly explained by the changing hormone levels in their body. Such feelings may, however, be due to the strain of being in the hospital or in an unfamiliar environment; some mothers desperately want to return home so that they can be with their partner and in their own surroundings. Provided a doctor has checked that all is well with you and the baby, there is no reason why you shouldn't go home earlier than planned if you want to.

Other mothers find coming home stressful

in itself, especially if the house is untidy or disorganized and there is work to do. Visitors can also prove too much at times, especially if you were wanting some time to yourself. Don't be afraid of saying "I must rest now" when the baby has gone to sleep. At least make a rule that visitors make the tea or coffee and clear up the dishes afterwards.

Occasionally a mother continues to feel depressed or weepy after the birth of a baby, and may need to talk this over with someone who understands. A doctor or counselor may well be able to offer help and support, as well as sympathy.

Week 3

Month: Dates:

MON

TUES

WED

THURS

FRI

SAT

SUN

Notes

DRESSING BABY

All-in-one stretch suits with snaps at the front and crotch are the easiest for changing a baby, and they are also very warm. Many parents prefer these to the old-fashioned nightgowns which tend to ride up and leave the baby exposed; however, you can now get gowns which tie or have snaps at the bottom.

With all clothes, make sure sleeves are not too tight, that there is plenty of room for him to kick, and that there is nothing itchy next to his skin.

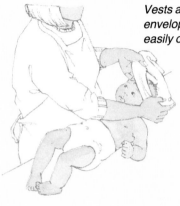

Vests and tops with large envelop necks slip easily over baby's head.

Once the vest is over the baby's head, gently ease each arm into the armholes – do not resort to force!

First clothes and equipment

There is such a bewildering array of goods on sale for the new mother and baby that it may seem hard to know what to buy, especially if you are short of space at home. Bear in mind that friends and relatives will give you clothes for the baby, so just buy the essential garments to begin with and wait to see what else you need.

You must have several changes of clothes for your baby because diapers often leak and some dribbling and regurgitating of milk is inevitable. Some babies also suck their sleeves and leave them wringing wet. Clothes made of cotton rather than artificial fibers are best for a very young baby and usually wash well. Bear in mind that colored clothes can look better than white, especially after a few washes; white can get very grubby and any yellow milk-stains are hard to remove. Don't buy too many clothes in very small sizes as these will quickly be outgrown. You can always dress your baby in something that's a little too big for him.

Some equipment can also be considered essential, and other items can wait until later, once you assess your real needs. The basic immediate requirements are some form of transportation and somewhere for the baby to sleep. Think carefully about transportation as carriages and strollers are very expensive. You have to choose a carriage or stroller designed for young babies and a specially designed baby car seat. If you do not travel by car, a carrier or sling may see you through until you can use a lighter, folding buggy.

There is no need for a full-sized crib for several months, so it may be worth waiting and choosing exactly the crib you want. If you inherit or buy any of these items second-hand, always check that they are safe. If you buy a carriage or stroller new, make sure that it comes with some kind of warranty for all major parts.

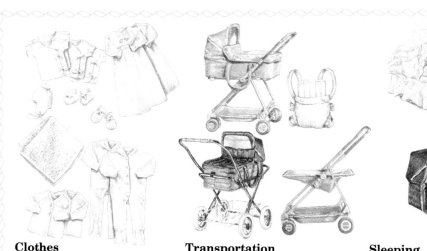

Clothes

- ☐ at least four undershirts
- ☐ four to six stretch suits or nightgowns
- ☐ woollen booties, mittens and hat for a winter baby
- ☐ a shawl for wrapping and swaddling the baby
- ☐ three woollen cardigans or jackets

Transportation

The choice of equipment for transporting your baby includes an all-in-one system incorporating a portable bassinet on a carriage frame, a bassinet or traveller body on a foldaway transporter chassis, a stroller and a sling or baby carrier.

Sleeping

In the early weeks a Moses basket is both pretty and useful, as you can carry it around the house, but it cannot be safely secured in a car. You can use a portable bassinet for the baby to sleep in, or he can sleep in a carriage.

See Week 4 for Diapers

See Week 5 for Bathing Baby

See Week 11 for Choosing a Crib

Week 4

MON

TUES

WED

THURS

FRI

SAT

SUN

Notes

■ SLEEP POSITIONS

Most babies have a favorite position to sleep in, but, until they are old enough to roll over, they will depend on you to put them down so that they are comfortable. There is a slight danger of a baby choking if she is lying on her back, so put her on her side or stomach.

If you have a restless baby, it may help to swaddle her in a shawl or receiving blanket before you put her to sleep. She will feel more secure being swaddled for the first few weeks as she has only just left the womb.

To swaddle your baby, fold the receiving blanket crosswise into a triangle and lay her on it with the longest side at shoulder level. Place her right arm comfortably across her chest and bring the right-hand corner of the blanket over, tucking it firmly under her bottom. Repeat with the left arm, bringing the left side of the blanket across and tucking it behind her back. After about five weeks old, leave her hands free so that she can put her fingers or fist to her mouth.

If your baby sleeps on her side, roll up a blanket or shawl and wedge it behind her back to stop her rolling over.

Many babies sleep most comfortably on their stomach. There is no need to swaddle a slightly older baby.

Diapers

New mothers are often uncertain whether to opt for disposable diapers or cloth ones. Choosing cloth diapers seems a big initial outlay, and you also need a bucket for soaking, diaper liners, plastic pants and diaper pins. However, cloth diapers do work out cheaper in the long run, and many mothers find them more efficient at keeping a young baby dry.

The decision will depend largely on your circumstances. If you have an automatic washing machine and have space outside or inside to dry things, then cloth diapers may well be best. Some mothers find that cloth diapers are more absorbent, especially for a small breast-fed baby, and that they therefore have fewer baby clothes to wash. Cloth diapers may seem difficult to put on at first, but it doesn't take long once you're used to it – even in the dark in the middle of the night. You will probably have been shown one or several ways to fold a diaper while in the hospital: the kite fold, the triple fold, or without pins for a newborn baby.

If you don't have much space and washing is a problem, disposable diapers are the more practical solution. Try out several different kinds to see which you like best and make sure they don't irritate your baby's bottom. Elasticated legs are a good idea for small babies. Modern all-in-one disposables are very absorbent and are less bulky than cloth diapers.

Changing diapers can be done quickly if you can have everything in one place. You can make an ideal changing table from an old dresser that is waist-high on which you can put a changing pad. This saves having to bend down all the time to change diapers, which can put a strain on your back. Make sure that cleaning materials, cream and fresh diapers and liners are to hand. If you are using cloth diapers, keep the sterilizing bucket nearby and drop in the dirty diaper.

Night changing

At night, have everything you need laid out ready and cut down diaper changes to a minimum. You can get specially thick cloth diapers or disposables, and one-way diaper liners, for night-time use.

Many babies soil their diapers after a feeding. If you change the diaper first, the baby may go back to sleep after her feeding but with a dirty diaper; if you change it after the feeding, you may wake her up. But if you change a diaper quickly and keep the room dark, you are unlikely to disturb her very much and this may prevent her getting sore. Breast-fed babies are much less prone to diaper rash.

□ Use the cloth or disposable diaper to wipe the baby's bottom and then use absorbent cotton and warm water or a baby wipe to cleanse her skin. Take care to clean in the folds.

□ If there are any signs of soreness, use zinc and castor oil cream or another preparation to protect the skin. If a rash is not helped by a diaper rash cream, ask your doctor for advice.

□ Put on a clean diaper, fastening the sticky tape of a disposable diaper at the front. (Remember to wipe a girl from front to back to prevent bacteria, spreading from the anus, infecting the vagina.)

Week 5

Month: Dates:

MON

TUES

WED

THURS

FRI

SAT

SUN

Notes

By five or six weeks your new baby should be rewarding you with his first smile. Often when you are changing his diaper, he will look at you and study your face first, before breaking into a smile; you need to talk to him and give him a chance to respond.

A small baby at this stage will also "fix" his gaze on an object and follow it if it moves. The human face is what he most enjoys looking at and he will "fix" on your face for quite long periods.

When your newborn baby hears your voice he may turn his eyes towards the sound and will follow your face if you hold it close to his. He will watch you while you are speaking to him and may even open and close his mouth in imitation. He may stop crying as soon as you pick him up and talk to him.

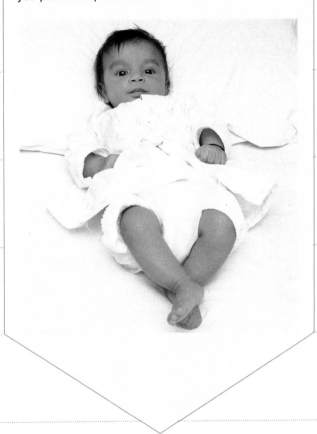

■ **DON'T FORGET** Note down the date of your baby's first smile. Make an appointment for postpartum checkup if you don't already done so.

Bathing baby

Once a baby enjoys his bath it makes a delightful form of exercise for him. It is probably the only opportunity he gets to move his limbs with all his clothes off, especially in the winter. But bathing the baby can initially be a traumatic time for some new parents, especially if he screams, writhes and thrashes. Although you may have been shown how to bath your baby in the hospital, it can all seem rather different when you are at home. New babies do not need bathing every day, especially if they hate it. "Sponge bathing" will keep a baby clean in the early weeks if you can't give a bath. But try to bath him every few days to give him a chance to get used to it.

It helps to get everything ready first and to bath the baby somewhere where you will be comfortable; keep the room warm. A baby bath with stand brings the baby to the right height, but you could bath him on a firm table or other surface provided you do not turn your back, even for a moment. A wooden shelf placed over the big bath saves you having to lift a heavy bath of water far.

Make sure the water is about body temperature (it shouldn't feel hot or cold if you dip your elbow in) and hold the baby firmly, talking to him all the time. Many babies dislike getting dressed or undressed but are quiet in the water.

If your baby really does hate the bath, you can try having him in the bath with you provided there's someone else around to help pass the baby in and out. Let your bath water cool right down and have it shallow enough so that, when the baby is resting on your lap, it is not too deep for him. Most babies will find the skin-to-skin contact reassuring and this may help them get over their fear of the water.

Many parents find that a bath makes a pleasant end to the day, and also tires the baby out, so that after a bath and feeding he is ready to be settled for the night. Evening bathtime also enables fathers to be involved with the baby. But if you have older children, the morning may be a better time for bathing him; he will then settle down for a long morning sleep.

A sponge bath

Hold the baby on his back in your lap with his head between your knees and gently clean his face with absorbent cotton and warm water. Wipe his eyes first, from the bridge of the nose outwards, using a different piece for each eye so as not to spread any infection. Wipe around the ears with absorbent cotton. Then clean up the rest of his face to remove traces of milk or saliva which may irritate his skin. Pat dry with a soft towel. Wash his hands with absorbent cotton and warm water. Finally, clean his bottom with water or a baby wipe, dry thoroughly and put on a fresh diaper.

☐ With your baby wrapped in a towel, hold his head over the bath and wash his scalp gently with your free hand. Pat it dry.

☐ Just support him and let him splash for a few minutes, rather than soaping him immediately.

☐ Have a warm towel ready to wrap the baby in when he comes out, as small babies get cold very quickly.

See Week 4 for Diapers

Week 6

Month: _____ Dates: _____

MON

TUES

WED

THURS

FRI

SAT

SUN

Notes

ROUTINE LABORATORY TESTS

In the normal process of growing up, your child will probably need various kinds of medical services, ranging from routine physical examinations (see "Well-baby examinations," p. 19) to laboratory tests to surgery. Some of the laboratory tests that are commonly performed are listed below. Except for tuberculosis testing, most of these tests are not routinely done unless your doctor feels there is some reason they should be.

Tuberculosis screening (the Tine test) Most pediatricians recommend that it be done every two to three years.

Cholesterol screening Testing for blood cholesterol is usually only done in cases where there is a family history of heart attacks, although increasing numbers of pediatricians are performing this test as a matter of course.

Urine screening This involves a urine analysis to detect bacterial infections, and is usually only done in children who have had urinary tract infections in the past.

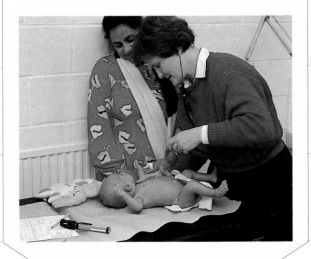

DON'T FORGET You should make an appointment for your baby's next well-baby visit, if your haven't already.

The postpartum checkup

You will need to have a postpartum checkup six weeks after the birth. This may be done at the clinic where you had your baby or at your obstetrician's office.

The doctor will feel your abdomen to check that the womb has returned to its normal size and may check your weight and blood pressure. You will be asked if you have had any unusual pain, bleeding or discharge; it is quite normal for the lochia, the usual discharge after the baby's birth, to still be present and some mothers who are not breast-feeding may already have had a menstrual period.

Any scars from tears or episiotomies may be examined, especially if they are causing discomfort. If you still have pain in the site of your episiotomy, make sure the doctor checks to ensure that it is not infected. The doctor may also look at your breasts and nipples if you are having problems with breast-feeding. The doctor will usually discuss contraception with you at this visit.

The postpartum checkup gives you the opportunity to discuss any worries you might have. You may be anxious about sex if you have either tried intercourse and found it painful or have not yet attempted it, which is very common. Remember that your health is vital to the wellbeing of your baby. If you have problems or worries, don't be afraid to talk about them.

Obtaining a birth certificate

There will be many occasions in the coming years when you will need a certified birth certificate for your child; for example, when you register your child for school or apply for a passport. In order to obtain a certified birth certificate with an official raised seal, you must write either to your state Bureau of Vital Statistics (usually located in the state capital) or to the registry office in the town or borough where your child was born. In your letter, you should supply the following details: child's name, date and place of birth, father's name, mother's maiden name, and your current address. The fee for certificates varies, but is usually no more than $5.

Postpartum exercises

Your doctor will probably recommend some simple exercises to help you get back into shape after your baby was born. However, many mothers find they are so busy after the birth that they are tempted to give up doing them after a week or two. It is important that you carry on with these exercises as they will help you keep fit and make you better able to enjoy your baby. Below is a reminder of some of the basic exercises which you should do several times a day.

For your stomach muscles:
☐ Lie on your back on the floor, knees bent and hands on upper chest. Lift head and shoulders off the floor, keeping your waist and back on the floor: look at your knees. Then relax.

For your back:
☐ Lie face downwards on the floor, arms behind your back, clasping hands loosely. Lift head and shoulders off the floor. Then relax.

For your pelvic floor muscles:
☐ Tighten the muscles to pull up your vagina and anus towards your body. Hold for five seconds and then relax. If you are not sure that you are tightening the right muscles, try interrupting the flow of urine next time you go for a pee.

Do this exercise regularly; it is very important as it will help you avoid some 'women's complaints' later on, such as prolapse of the uterus, or incontinence.

See Week 7 for well-baby examinations

Week 7

Month: _____   Dates: _____

MON

TUES

WED

THURS

FRI

SAT

SUN

Notes

Babies can see immediately after birth, although they can initially only focus within a very narrow range. A baby can focus on objects held within 10 inches of his face – about the distance you will naturally hold your baby when talking to him. Despite his limited focusing, a baby will flinch or try to protect himself if you move something very rapidly towards his face.

Your baby cannot see colors at all to begin with. As the first colors he will respond to will be bright ones, give him brightly colored objects to look at.

Well-baby examinations

Well-baby visits to the doctor during the first year are extremely important. At these visits, your baby is given careful physical examinations, routine tests, and those necessary immunizations. These visits also provide an excellent opportunity for you to ask questions, air your concerns, and get the reassurance that you need that your baby is progressing well. The first visit is usually scheduled the first two weeks after birth. Some doctors require at least three more visits in the first year and two in the second; others like to see infants on a monthly basis for the first six months. Of course, you should not hesitate to phone your doctor between visits if your baby becomes ill or you have additional concerns.

At each well-baby visit, you usually have to undress the baby to be weighed, so it is important to put him in clothes that will come off and on easily; also take a spare diaper in case you need to change him. The doctor or his assistant will enter the baby's weight both in their records and in a book which you keep with you. The weight gains shown in the chart below are only an average; most babies will grow more slowly one week, to be compensated for by a larger weight gain the next. A baby's weight may also vary according to whether he has just passed a bowel movement or not, so don't take each week's gain too seriously if the general trend is good.

Most doctors are supportive of breast-feeding and will give you advice if your breast-fed baby is not gaining weight satisfactorily or if you have other problems.

However, you may feel you need extra help or advice with breast-feeding, in which case you can ask the doctor for the number of the La Leche League chapter nearest you or look in the white pages. These counselors are trained mothers who have breast-fed their own babies and will be dedicated to helping you to continue to breast-feed if this is what you want.

The doctor will advise you about giving vitamin supplements or fluoride drops to help create strong, healthy teeth. In addition to doing vision and hearing tests and developmental screening, they will also help with problems such as colic or lack of sleep and first illnesses such as colds.

If you have any queries about your baby's appearance, don't be afraid to discuss these with the doctor. Doctors are used to seeing newborn babies and will be able to reassure you that everything is normal.

It may be useful to make a list of all the questions that you want to ask the doctor before you go, so you don't forget any of them.

See Week 1 for Feeding Your Baby

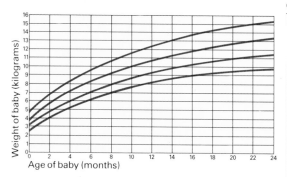

Weight of baby (kilograms) / **Age of baby (months)**

Recording weight

The weight gain chart shows typical growth lines for four babies of varying birth weight. Weight gain is rapid in the early months. The average weekly gain for a baby in the first three months is around 7 ounces, though a small baby may grow faster and a big baby more slowly. It then slows down but should follow a steady curve as he grows.

Week 8

Month: Dates:

MON

TUES

WED

THURS

FRI

SAT

SUN

Notes

HEAD CONTROL

Your baby will gradually learn to control her head and be able to lift it for longer periods. You may find that she bumps her head against your shoulder while you are carrying her as she practises her head control.

When lying on her stomach she will start to lift her head up at a 45-degree angle and look straight ahead for a few minutes at a time. She will begin to be able to turn her head from side to side when you put her down to sleep. Until your baby has gained full head control, continue to support her head when carrying her.

By two months your baby will probably be able to lift her head up for several minutes, using her forearms as support.

By three or four months she will be able to do "press-ups" and may also make crawling movements with her arms and legs.

DON'T FORGET Checking your baby's weight regularly will reassure you that feeding is going well.

First immunizations

At eight weeks your baby will be due for her first set of immunizations against potentially life-threatening diseases. By immunizing your child, you are not only protecting her but, by reducing the number of people who can catch such diseases, you are also protecting your next baby and other people's children who have not been immunized. Because diseases like polio and diphtheria have become so rare, some people have become careless about having their children immunized as they think that it is not important. If fewer people have their children immunized, it becomes more likely that these diseases will reappear.

The usual vaccines given at this age are the polio vaccine – nowadays given by mouth – and the "triple vaccine" for diphtheria, tetanus and whooping cough (pertussis). The repeat vaccines are given at four months and then around six months. It is important that your child has all three sets to be fully protected.

The vaccines should not cause any side-effects, except perhaps for a reddish patch at the site of the injection and occasionally a temperature. The whooping cough vaccine can very rarely cause serious side-effects, such as a fit or convulsion leading to brain damage. It is important though to remember that whooping cough is a serious disease which itself can lead to brain damage or even death. You will be advised not to have the whooping cough vaccine if there is a history of epilepsy or convulsions in the baby's immediate family or if she has suffered a fit herself.

Tuberculosis is still common in some parts of the country and children in these areas should have routine screening examinations (once a year up to four years, then every other year after that). All adult family members of children with positive TB tests should also be tested. Be guided by your doctor.

Around 15 months you will be advised to have your baby immunized against measles. Some parents may think that measles is not a serious disease, and that it is not worth immunizing their child. However, measles can be a very unpleasant illness and sometimes has serious consequences, such as ear infections and pneumonia. When your baby is immunized you can discuss the measles vaccine too.

If you have any worries about the baby's immunizations do discuss these with your family doctor or pediatrician, who will be able to give you all the facts and reassure you if necessary.

IMMUNIZATION/VACCINATION TIMETABLE		
Age	**Immunization**	**Method**
2 months	Diphtheria Whooping cough Tetanus	(DTP) Injection
	Polio	Drops by mouth
4 months	DTP Polio	Injection Drops by mouth
6 months	DTP Polio	Injection Drops by mouth
15 months	Measles Mumps Rubella	Injection
18 months	DTP Polio	Injection Drops by mouth

Finger games
Diaper-changing times are a good opportunity for tickling and blowing raspberries on your baby's tummy, and letting her kick her legs and wave her arms. Babies of three months will enjoy traditional tickling games such as these:

☐ "Round and round the garden, like a teddy bear – one step, two steps, tickle you under there!" (Circling the baby's palm with your index finger, two "walking" steps up her arm, then tickling her in the armpit.)

☐ "This little piggy went to market, this little piggy stayed at home, this little piggy had roast beef, and this little piggy had none. And *this* little piggy went "Wee – wee – wee – wee", all the way home!" (Taking each of her fingers in turn, ending with the little finger, and then tickling all the way up her arm.)

Week 9

Month: Dates:

MON

TUES

WED

THURS

FRI

SAT

SUN

Notes

Your baby will now be spending more time awake during the daytime and you will be wondering how to divert him. From six weeks on you can sit him in a bouncing cradle and move him from room to room with you so he can watch you as you work. Never put the cradle on a high surface as the baby's movements could easily shift it.

With the baby in a carrier or sling, you can keep him close to you while you prepare vegetables or do other tasks around the house. Many parents find a sling particularly valuable for carrying a crying baby around, leaving both arms free while at the same time giving the baby comfort and security.

You can also take your baby round the house from room to room with you in his portable bassinet or infant seat so that you can sing or talk to him while you work.

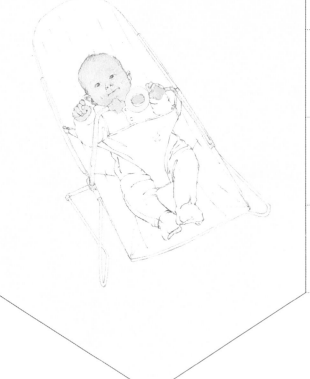

You and your partner

After the baby is born you may find that you have to readjust aspects of your relationship with your partner. If you have both been going out to work and shared equally in household tasks, you may find that things are different now that you are at home with your baby. Your partner may assume that, because you are at home and not working, responsibility for household tasks falls more on your shoulders. If you have always played

a domestic role, you may feel that it is all too much to cope with at once and may find that, with the baby to look after, you are not getting all the shopping, cooking and housework done as before.

In the early weeks you may be totally preoccupied with the baby, and your partner may not understand why you have so little time to talk to him or be with him. Even though he realizes that the baby's demands must come first, he may start to feel left out or be worried that things will never be the same again between you.

A partner really has two choices when he has a new baby. He can either involve himself with the baby, take over some of the tasks, like changing diapers, bathing the baby, feeding a bottle-fed baby and comfort-ing him when he cries – or he can sit back and let the mother do the major part. If he involves himself with the baby, gets up at night and early in the morning, he will realize how demanding a baby is and will better understand why his partner is so tired – especially since she has been through a pregnancy and childbirth too. He may also often feel too tired to make love! If, however, he does not involve himself with the baby, he may feel left out and might become resentful of his partner's tiredness and seeming lack of interest in him – and wish that things could get "back to normal" as soon as possible.

Time together

It is important that you and your partner try to create some time for each other and that you do talk things over. Once the baby is old enough to be left with a trusted babysitter you can go out by yourselves, or you may be able to find time to be together when the baby is asleep, postponing chores until later.

Resuming sex

Sex is often a problem at this time. After the discomforts of pregnancy and the weeks immediately after the birth, many men see no reason why making love should be postponed any longer. Many women, however, continue to be anxious that they may not feel comfortable or they may want affection and cuddles rather than passion.

Unless a couple can talk openly about their feelings, resentment can build up. If sex becomes a real problem, it can help to talk about it to your doctor or a counselor. A permanent loss of interest in sex can be a symptom of depression but is perfectly understandable so soon after giving birth. Some mothers are simply afraid of how sex after childbirth will feel, especially if they have a scar, or they fear that their partners will no longer find them attractive. They are often pleased to find that they enjoy it as much as ever.

See Week 14 for Leaving Baby at Home

See Week 21 for Fathers

Week 10

Month: _____   Dates: _____

MON
_____
_____

TUES
_____
_____

WED
_____
_____

THURS
_____
_____

FRI
_____
_____

SAT
_____
_____

SUN
_____
_____

Notes
_____

■ COPING WITH CRYING

Crying is the only way a small baby can communicate her feelings. A baby usually has a reason for crying and, although at first it is difficult to distinguish between different cries, you will soon begin to recognize variations and to guess her needs more accurately (see Week 19). However, some young babies do cry more than others, seemingly for comfort or distraction.

If your baby cries a lot, she will need to be soothed. Try putting her in a sling and carrying her round with you: you can make a sling out of a large shawl if necessary. Holding her firmly against your shoulder and rocking her or walking up and down are good ways of soothing a crying baby, especially if she tends to thrash around.

You can buy a battery-operated or hand-cranked swing for your baby. These can swing for some time after you start them in motion and can be soothing for a baby. You can also use a rocking cradle.

If you have a baby who constantly continues to cry after you have tried everything, by all means consult your pediatrician. It may be that your baby has colic; the crying could also be a symptom of some more serious problem. In either case, you need the advice and support of your physician.

Baby's first illness

You will be very lucky if you get through the baby's first few months without a minor illness – even though a breast-fed baby is protected by your antibodies to illnesses which you have had. Almost all babies will pick up a cold in the early months of their life, and occasionally something more serious. A cold is not usually serious for a baby, but it can cause problems in feeding if her nose is very blocked and she cannot suck well. If this happens, the doctor may recommend inhalant capsules to enable her to breathe more easily. At night, try propping up the head of the baby's crib or basket or use a cool-mist humidifier to relieve some of her congestion. A humidifier is much safer than a steam vaporizer because it uses room-temperature; consult your doctor or your pharmacist about this.

Many babies have a slight rash called a milk rash which does no harm at all, and looks like tiny pimples on the skin. A red, scaly rash, which may weep and irritate, is more likely to be eczema, which can be caused or exacerbated by an allergy. Diaper rash is caused by bacteria in the baby's stools breaking down the urine into ammonia, which damages the skin. A very red blotchy rash in the diaper area which persists despite applying the usual creams may be caused by thrush; this can only be cured by a fungicidal cream which your doctor can prescribe. Thrush can also appear as white spots in the mouth or soreness on the nipples.

Many babies cry a great deal in the early weeks. Some have a

Taking temperature and giving medicine
You can take the baby's temperature with a thermometer held under the arm. Put the bulb of the thermometer in her armpit and hold her arm against her side for two minutes. You can do this while feeding to distract her if she struggles. You can alternatively use a fever strip, which changes colour depending on the baby's temperature, though this gives a less accurate reading.

Giving medicine by spoon can be tricky, both with a small baby who is not used to spoons, and with a larger one who dislikes the taste. If you cannot get the baby to take medicine off an ordinary spoon, try giving it in a special tube-shaped, non-spill medicine "spoon". You could even try using a dropper or syringe which you should be able to get from your pharmacist or doctor; simply drop or squirt the medicine into the baby's mouth. Keep these in sterilizing fluid between uses.

You may be able to fool an older baby by giving her a spoonful of food, then the medicine.

pattern of "evening crying", others may have crying spells at other times of day or even all day long. Many such babies are said to suffer from colic, although nobody really knows what colic is. Sometimes colic seems to be related to feeding and many mothers – and doctors too – assume that it is caused by indigestion-type pains. However, many colicky babies appear to need very little sleep and their crying seems to be related more to lack of sleep than feeding.

If you have a baby who cries a lot it is hard not to worry that something is seriously wrong. However, colicky babies usually gain weight well, are healthy and grow out of their colicky spells by three to six months. The parents of colicky babies are often more in need of help, as this can be a stressful time. A baby who is really ill, surprisingly, cries little but seems listless, loses her appetite, may not gain weight well and/or may have vomiting and diarrhea; she will not be interested in what is going on around her. A baby who does not smile when she is usually a lively, smiling baby, may well be ill.

Take your baby to the doctor if she runs a high temperature, is breathing rapidly, vomits large amounts of milk, has watery diarrhea, has a bad cough or appears in pain. Although most new parents worry about their baby, the fear that they might appear to be over-anxious can deter them from taking the baby to the doctor. However, most parents' instincts will tell them when something is really wrong and, even if it turns out not to be serious, no doctor will mind seeing a small baby.

Week 11

Month: Dates:

MON

TUES

WED

THURS

FRI

SAT

SUN

Notes

■ COMFORT OBJECTS

Your baby may become very attached to a "comforter" such as a special soft toy or a blanket. As long as he uses these only when needed and does not withdraw from other activities, they will do no harm and may be a bonus in helping him to go to sleep without tears. Try to ensure that the blanket or toy is one that does not shed too much fluff or hair.

If you have used a pacifier your baby may rely on one to get him to sleep. This won't do him any harm either, but if you want to break the habit, it might be easier to provide another security object now rather than later. Some babies wake frequently in the night because the pacifier drops out and they need you to come and pop it back in!

Some babies suck their thumbs or fingers for comfort and this habit is almost impossible to stop. Many parents welcome this habit as it usually means peaceful bedtimes, and there is no need to discourage it, provided he sucks his thumb mainly to get to sleep, and not too much in the day. A young baby cannot keep his thumb in his mouth in the early weeks.

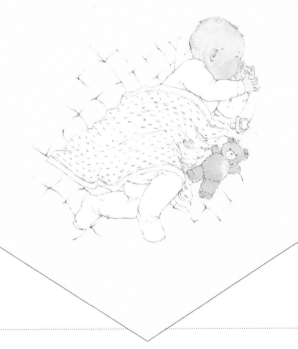

Sleep patterns

Most parents hope that by about three or four months their baby will be sleeping through the night, but many are not. Some babies may have slept through on occasions but then, perhaps because of teething problems or a cold, develop a habit of waking regularly again in the night.

Sleeping through the night
Babies vary a lot in their need for sleep and some are lighter sleepers than others. It does no harm to the baby if he wakes several times a night but, if you are exhausted, you may feel that you are not enjoying your baby as you should.

It may help to make a clear division between night and day. During the day naps may be taken in a carriage or portable crib downstairs, but at night only in his crib in a darkened room. In the daytime you might go immediately to your baby when he wakes and cries, but at night give him a few minutes to settle down first. If your baby is a light sleeper, make sure he is not disturbed by

Choosing a crib
Cribs come in different shapes and sizes; study your own needs before you buy. You can buy a large crib which converts into a child's bed; these may be good value in the long run, unless you already have suitable single beds. Most basic cribs have adjustable heights for the mattress – high for lifting a small baby in and out, and low to prevent a toddler climbing out.

All cribs must meet with Consumer Product Safety Standards Commission safety standards. These standards cover such points as drop sides; check that the mechanism works smoothly and that the baby cannot pinch his fingers in it. Check that the crib bars are not wide enough apart for the baby to get his head wedged in them. If you buy a second-hand crib, check that the mattress fits the base exactly and that the crib is painted with lead-free paint.

traffic sounds or by the family going to bed. Light sleepers do better in their own room.

Every child – and adult too – wakes briefly at regular intervals during the night. If nothing disturbs you, you go straight back to sleep with no memory of having woken. Many babies wake briefly and, finding themselves alone, immediately cry. If they have gone to sleep sucking at the breast or bottle they may cry for its return. Such babies may go on demanding night-time feedings long after they have ceased to be necessary.

Encourage your baby to learn to fall asleep on his own in his crib. If he cries, go back in after a few minutes, resettle him, and leave him to fall asleep. Many parents find that the baby cries for a night or two but soon starts waking less frequently. Give water when he wakes at night, instead of milk, to discourage waking.

Some parents find it easier to settle the baby if they take him straight into their bed. Provided they know this habit may be hard to break, and do not resent sharing a bed, this can be the answer to children's sleep problems till they feel old enough to sleep alone.

Some babies wake very early in the morning. Check that the room is warm enough and that curtains exclude light effectively. If you cannot juggle his bedtime so that he sleeps later in the morning, at least put interesting things in the crib for him to look at or play with, such as an "activity center".

See Week 37 for Sleep Problems

Week 12

Month: Dates:

MON

TUES

WED

THURS

FRI

SAT

SUN

Notes

SOCIAL DEVELOPMENT

By three months your baby will already be a social person, taking her greatest pleasure out of her relationship with you. As early as six weeks some babies are starting to coo in response to your voice and will lie on your lap carrying out a kind of "conversation" as you talk to them. By three months she will laugh when you tickle or talk to her and will love being tickled when you change her diaper.

At this age your baby is likely to stop crying when she hears your voice or when you pick her up. She also responds to other people who pay her attention with smiles and by kicking and waving her arms, although her greatest enthusiasm is likely to be reserved for her mother.

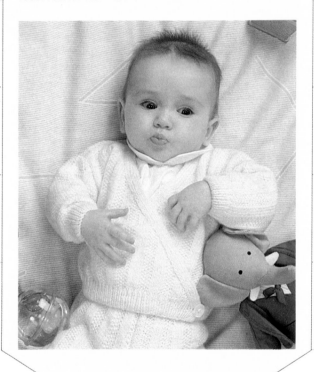

DON'T FORGET It is important to continue with your pelvic floor exercises (see Week 6).

Getting out and about

Getting out of the house may seem a massive undertaking at first. A short trip to the grocery store may not be too much of a problem but if you are going further afield you may wonder if it is worth the effort. The baby needs to be fed and changed; then all her equipment – a change of clothes, spare diapers, bottles if you are bottle-feeding – needs to be packed. By the time you are ready to go, she may need feeding again!

It helps if you keep a bag ready containing everything you need, so that you just have to

pick it up as you leave the house. If you are traveling by car, always keep a spare change in the car so that you won't be caught without diapers or clothes. Even if you usually use cloth diapers, disposables are handy for going out so that you don't have to carry a bag of dirty diapers around with you. Always wrap a soiled disposable diaper in a sealed plastic bag before disposing of it.

Breast-feeding mothers have an advantage over bottle-feeding mothers because they don't need to take feeding equipment with them, but some women are anxious about having to breast-feed their baby in public. With a few exceptions, there are far too few public places in which to feed babies comfortably and privately. However, it is possible to breast-feed discreetly if you wear

suitable clothing.

If you take your baby out by car, it is important to get the car fitted with special anchoring straps to hold the car seat in place on the back seat, or to have one of the special baby seats which locks into ordinary seat-belts. Babies have been killed when thrown out of their bassinets in road accidents. Never be tempted to hold your baby in either the front or back seat of a car. In an accident the force would send her straight through the glass. And never put an adult seat-belt around both of you. Information is available from the National Highway Traffic Safety Administration or Physicians for Automotive Safety (see Useful Addresses).

Using public transportation

If you travel by public transportation, it is easiest if you take a stroller which folds up or else carry the baby in a sling or carrier. It is difficult to get a portable bassinet on a bus, but you may manage better on a train.

Your clothes

As a new mother you will find it hard to look good and feel comfortable at the same time. Buy a few well-chosen clothes which will get a lot of wear – for many mothers this is essential as they are still too big to get back into pre-pregnancy clothes and are tired of their maternity clothes. Buy clothes that can be washed and ironed easily – they frequently get dirty when caring for a baby.

Clothes that are practical and comfortable do not have to be dowdy – looking good will help you to feel that you are coping as well as making you feel attractive and well in yourself.

Breast-feeding mothers will want either front-opening clothes or loose tops which they can pull up to feed the baby more discreetly – and loose, comfortable skirts or slacks.

Week 13

Month: Dates:

MON

TUES

WED

THURS

FRI

SAT

SUN

Notes

LEARNING TO GRASP

Until your baby is about eight weeks old he will not be able to unclench his hands or take hold of anything. By two to two-and-a-half months, however, he will become fascinated by watching his hands moving and will move them in front of his face. By three months he will be very interested in "measuring" the distance between objects and him, which is when he begins reaching out and swiping at those within his reach.

By three to four months you will need to be on your guard because your baby will start to grab at everything within reach, and will have a preference for things which move and make a noise.

Many two-month-old babies will lie for long periods watching their hands move. They will also be fascinated by mobiles wafting in the air.

By three months your baby will take great pleasure in swiping with his fists at anything within reach.

Clothing and toys

Clothes for a growing baby

As your baby grows and you go out more together he will probably need more clothes. He may require warmer, thicker stretch suits or jogging suits for daytime wear in the winter, or larger woollen cardigans and sweaters. If it is cold, a snow suit will keep the baby warm and dry outdoors, without wrapping him under layers of blankets in a carriage (but see below).

Don't make the mistake of overdressing your baby, especially when he is in a warm house. As babies get bigger they do learn to adjust to warm or cold conditions. Always wrap him up warmly when going out in the cold, however; hats are very important as most of a baby's heat loss is through his head. When you come into a warm house again, always unwrap your baby, even if he is fast asleep. This may be a reason for using blankets rather than a snow suit, so that you disturb him as little as possible.

Many babies overheat easily and can readily develop a heat rash, so be sure not to put too many clothes on a summer baby, especially if the weather is hot. Babies have cold hands and feet most of the time, so feel the back of his neck if you want to check how warm he is overall.

First toys

Around the age of three months, your baby will start taking more interest in the objects around him. He will love to watch brightly colored mobiles; you can hang one over his changing mat and another in the kitchen or living room so he can look at it from his bouncing cradle. Your baby will start to reach out for things he can see and will enjoy swiping at an object dangled within his reach. A toy fixed to the bouncing cradle is a good idea at this age.

Rattles now start to come in too, although it will be another few weeks before your baby can actually grasp one and shake it in a controlled way. At this stage he is quite likely to bang his head with it or poke it in his eye. However, you can string rattles and other brightly colored objects across the crib so that he can look at and reach out for them while lying on his back. He will watch rattles with interest if you hold them and shake them near his face.

A baby of this age is probably too young to cuddle soft toys although he may respond to those that squeak or rattle. He will probably enjoy looking at colorful pictures though, so you can try tucking some cards between the mattress and the side of his crib or carriage.

Try hanging mobiles – especially musical ones – and bright objects above your baby's crib, changing mat or playmat.

At this age, babies enjoy exploring different textures, so give him toys that are soft and furry, smooth and squeaky, hard and cool.

Week 14

Month: Dates:

MON

TUES

WED

THURS

FRI

SAT

SUN

Notes

LEARNING TO ROLL

Your baby may start to roll from her back to her side at this time, and it is doubly important that you do not leave her, even for a moment, lying down on the changing table or on the bed.

When lying on her tummy, she may make "swimming" movements with her arms and legs. And if you hold her upright on your knee, she will enjoy "bouncing" and taking some of her weight on her legs.

Once your baby can roll over, it won't matter which way you put her down at night. You may lie her on her back and later find her on her stomach. Occasionally, though, a baby who has learned to roll from stomach to back may get stuck, and wake up crying. If she does this, you can try wedging a blanket down the side of the crib to prevent her rolling over.

Some babies become mobile through rolling over and over long before they learn to crawl. If you have an active baby, you will need to adopt some of the safety measures in Weeks 15 and 38, as a rolling baby can move a surprising distance in a short space of time. In particular, beware of your baby rolling off a bed, chair or other raised surface or rolling towards dangerous objects such as a fire or ironing board.

Once your baby has learned to roll over you may need to alter some habits such as changing her diaper on a raised surface.

Leaving baby at home

By the time your baby has turned three months old you should feel ready to start going out and doing some of the things you did before she was born, even if it is only a trip to the cinema or a restaurant in the evening, or to have your hair cut during the day. The first time you leave your baby and go out can be rather alarming – many mothers feel as if they have inadvertently left something behind!

You don't necessarily have to go out with your partner. Sometimes it can be very refreshing to go out alone or with friends for an evening, confidently leaving the baby with her father.

The baby's feeding
If you are breast-feeding, you can express milk to leave for your baby in a bottle. Expressed breast-milk will keep in a sterile container in the refrigerator for forty-eight hours or, if you can't express enough at once, you can freeze a little at a time for a few days before you go out and store it in the freezer. It is quite safe to add a little to already frozen milk kept in a bottle in the freezer.

You can buy simple hand-operated breast pumps if you cannot manage the technique of expressing by hand; these need to be carefully sterilized like all other feeding equipment. Some mothers find that they cannot "let down" their milk when using a pump; it can help to use a pump to express from one side while the baby is feeding at the other breast. Expressed breast-milk often looks thin and watery or may even separate on standing; this doesn't mean that it has gone bad, and the milk will return to normal consistency when it is warmed up.

If you are bottle-feeding, it is easy to make up a bottle ready for the babysitter or your partner to give to your baby.

Fathers
It can be hard for the father to involve himself very much with the baby in the early weeks, especially if you are breast-feeding, because you are always there and sometimes seem to be the only person who can pacify her. But it will help the father make a firm relationship with the baby if he is sometimes left in sole charge, while you spend an evening out with friends. You can also leave the baby with your partner for a few hours on the weekends, while you make a shopping trip or have your hair cut – anything you can't do with the baby there.

Even if you are breast-feeding, it may be a good idea to express milk so that the father can give a bottle at night once in a while – although you have to be able to sleep through the baby's crying while he warms the bottle if this is to be worthwhile.

Fathers can sometimes take the baby off your hands by taking her out for a walk in the carriage or sling, or by taking her with him when he visits friends or does some errands. Many men complain that there is nowhere for men to change diapers in stores or public places, as changing areas seem inevitably to be in the ladies' room – though there is always the park bench!

See Week 38 for Time to Yourself

About babysitters
It is of course important that you leave your baby with someone that you know and trust, and preferably someone familiar to the baby as well.

Make sure the babysitter knows how to warm and give a bottle. Remind her, for example, to loosen the top of the bottle to let air in and milk out! If she has not done it before, show her how to change a diaper too. Describe what you usually do when the baby wakes, and if she has any particular routine. It's a good idea to leave everything ready for the babysitter – a change of clothes laid out, a diaper already folded – in the place where it will be needed. Then you won't have to worry about the babysitter not being able to find something.

Always leave a number where you can be contacted in an emergency. If your babysitter is a young girl, she may like to have the number of another mother who is a neighbor.

Week 15

Month: _____ Dates: _____

MON

TUES

WED

THURS

FRI

SAT

SUN

Notes

Never leave within your baby's reach small objects which he could swallow, like coins, pins, buttons, small pieces of Lego or other bits from older children's toys. Do not give him anything sharp or too heavy to use as a rattle as he is likely to hit himself with it.

Never leave your baby unattended on a raised surface such as a changing mat or a bed as he can easily roll over and fall off.

If you have him on your lap at mealtimes, be careful that he does not suddenly reach out and grab at bowls or mugs of hot liquid standing on the table. Keep them well out of his reach.

If you have a pet, don't leave your baby unattended near the animal, who could try and sleep on his face or bite or scratch if the baby makes an unintended swipe.

Mugs and cups of hot liquid are among the commonest causes of burns and scalds to young children.

Baby in the daytime

As your baby approaches four months the range of things he can handle increases. At this age lying him on a mat on the floor, with rattles and other safe objects, can provide fairly long periods of contented play. He may enjoy lying on his stomach and lifting himself up on his hands to reach out for any toys or objects within his reach. He may even be able to move his body a little by rolling over.

At the stage that a baby enjoys being held and standing on his legs a baby bouncer may be a boon. It is excellent for a wakeful baby who wants to be with you, as you can hang it in a doorway where he can watch you working and feel part of what is going on. Use a baby bouncer only when the baby is able to support his head. At first he may just "stand" in the bouncer and perhaps shift from one foot to another or shuffle himself around, but he will soon learn to bounce and jump and even to dance. Never leave him unattended in a baby bouncer.

A baby of this age may also be old enough for a playpen. Although he is nowhere near mobile, a playpen provides a place in which his toys can be kept, and can even be a safe place to snuggle down if he is sleepy. You can hang interesting objects from the bars of a playpen or safety gate for the baby to swipe at. If there are other children or adults around, you won't have to worry about them treading on the baby or about pets possibly bothering him (see opposite). It also helps to get a baby used to a playpen long before he is mobile, or he may never accept the idea of it.

An activity center is a good investment at this age; it can be fixed to the bars of the crib or playpen. Many babies start to enjoy activity centres as early as three months and they will provide entertainment for months to come. Other popular toys for this stage are weighted objects which you can push over and which bounce back, and soft toys which squeak or make a sound. However, a baby of this age is happy to be 'entertained' without toys: he will get a lot of pleasure from walks, from bathtime games such as trickling water on his tummy and other gentle games (see Week 18). He may also enjoy hearing music on the radio. If you don't want to spend a lot of money on toys, you can make your own rattles, mobiles and cloth bricks from household materials.

Even if your baby is happy to spend some of his time playing with toys, remember that you are still his main source of pleasure and security so try to make time to talk to him and demonstrate how things work.

By four months it is probably safer for the baby to begin sleeping in a crib if he has been in a portable bassinet or Moses basket so far. You can put soft toys in the crib for your baby to play with on going to bed and waking, but make sure they do not have long strings or ribbons, or anything which the baby could swallow.

Toys that are simple to look at and explore can provide entertainment for your baby while you get on with household chores for a while.

An easily cleaned safety mat inside the play-pen is a good idea; these can usually be tied to the bars of the playpen. If you don't have one, you can use a washable rug or mat.

See Week 11 for Choosing a Crib

Week 16

Month: *Dates:*

MON

TUES

WED

THURS

FRI

SAT

SUN

Notes

SIGNS OF READINESS

Your baby is probably ready for solid foods when she is over three months old and:

☐ She starts to dribble – until she starts to make a lot of saliva she may find solids hard to cope with.

☐ She starts to chew on toys and other things.

☐ She starts to put her fingers and other objects in her mouth frequently.

☐ She shows less need or desire to suck for its own sake.

☐ She appears dissatisfied after a feeding or starts demanding extra feeding in twenty-four hours.

☐ She starts waking for a feeding in the night after having been sleeping through. Ask your doctor if you are unsure whether to increase the baby's milk or to start her on solids.

Never add salt to baby food that you are preparing. This can be harmful as the baby's kidneys are unable to cope with too much salt in their diet. Too much sugar can also be harmful to the baby, as well as encouraging a "sweet tooth". On the whole, babies who are not given any sweet things will not refuse wholesome, flavorful foods.

First solids

Around now you will probably be wondering when to start offering solid food. A young baby is unable to digest solid foods before at least three months, so don't be tempted to give solids earlier than this. Also, the earlier you give other foods, the more likely she is to develop an allergy to them. However, there will come a time when your baby starts to demand more food, and milk alone seems not to satisfy her. This often coincides with the baby wanting to put things in her mouth and also with a decline in her need to suck.

Start off with small quantities and don't give your baby too many new foods at a time – if one food seems to upset her, you will

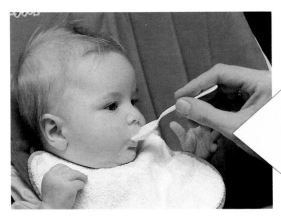

immediately know which it is. At this stage the foods are really "tastes" rather than meals, and you may have more success in giving them if you offer them to the baby when she is not too hungry. Some mothers sandwich first solids in the middle of the usual breast- or bottle-feeding; others find it easier to give a "snack" between meals. Either way, prepare yourself for this first experience with a bib, plenty of tissues or a facecloth – and do not be in a hurry.

If your baby doesn't take to solids at first, don't despair; she doesn't really need them yet. Just keep offering them and sooner or later she will get the idea. If she appears to spit them out, this may be only her initial attempts at swallowing.

You may find trying to prepare and feed such small amounts both frustrating and

time-consuming, especially if most of the food ends up on the baby's clothes! If you have a freezer, one tip is to sterilize a plastic ice tray and fill it with cubes of puréed food – you then only have to pop one or two out when needed. Prepared baby foods seem easy at this stage, but if your baby gets used to tasting at least some home-prepared foods from the beginning, this will help her not to become a fussy eater later on.

Many mothers are concerned about whether they should sterilize the equipment used in preparing foods for a small baby. If the food you use is cooked and freshly prepared, you do not have to sterilize the bowl, spoon and grater – they should be clean of course, and you can rinse them in boiling water before using them. If food is to be stored in the refrigerator (for up to 48 hours) you should sterilize the container.

First foods
It is important to remember that the baby is only used to swallowing liquids so make the first foods as sloppy as possible and let her suck them off the spoon. Do not try to hurry her.

What to give
The best foods to give your baby as first solids are gluten-free cereals, such as rice, or fruit purées. Rice needs to be ground and cooked – specially prepared 'baby rice' is available which can be used straight from the box – and mixed with the milk you are giving your baby, whether this is expressed breast-milk or formula. You can use water but this is too bland for the tastes of many babies.

Fruit needs to be cooked and puréed, except for banana, which needs to be very ripe and mashed till liquid. You can also give her purées of cooked vegetables such as carrots, potatoes and cauliflower, although some breast-fed babies are disappointed that the last two are not sweet.

See
Week 19 for
Baby's Meals

Week 17

Month: Dates:

MON

TUES

WED

THURS

FRI

SAT

SUN

Notes

FIRST SOUNDS

By three months most babies will be having limited "conversations" with their mothers. The baby will watch the mother's face and make cooing sounds, and if the mother repeats these back he will often try to imitate her expressions and sounds. He will become more adventurous once he gets used to, and enjoys, the sound of his own voice.

A little later he may start to look around for the source of a sound. He may look at something he can see, rather than what actually made the sound, unless the voice is one he knows. A baby of this age will "talk" most when spoken to by a familiar person, although some babies will babble away to toys or even the television. The sounds he makes usually indicate contentment and may lead to real laughter when he is particularly amused by some activity.

You will get hours of pleasure from your first conversations with your baby.

Meeting other mothers

If you are at home on your own with the baby there are going to be times when you feel at a loss for what to do. Perhaps the baby is unusually wakeful or irritable one day and you are unable to meet his demands. At such times it is a great help if you can go out and meet someone or do something enjoyable together. A trip round the park or to the shops on your own may help a little, but most mothers will want a purpose to their outing and would prefer to be able to talk to someone who understands.

Having a young child will often help you to meet fellow mothers as well as neighbors, including those without children. You may meet other mothers at the park or at

classes you attend with your baby. It is a good idea to arrange to take your babies for a walk together sometimes, so that you mothers can enjoy an adult conversation while the babies are being entertained by carriage-pushing.

If you were busy out at work before the baby was born, you may hardly have met any of your neighbors and other people in your community. They may stop to admire

the baby when you are out for a walk – take the opportunity to talk to them and perhaps invite them in for a cup of coffee. Once you know your neighbors, you many find that they can help out in emergencies – perhaps minding the baby for a short time while you pop out to the pharmacy on a wet evening. Equally, you might be able to help them, perhaps doing some shopping for an elderly neighbor while doing your own.

If you are not returning to work, you may find that there are other activities going on in the neighborhood in which you could become involved, such as helping to set up a new playgroup (see Week 49). The local school district may run adult education classes, where you can brush up on sewing or cooking or learn a language. Some of them even have a nursery for young children. Or you may be able to join an evening class and meet other people in your area.

Socializing
You could fix a regular morning or afternoon a week for mothers to meet for tea or coffee in one another's houses. You can organize this through your local health clinic – or make your own informal arrangement.

Social activities
□ In many areas there are local mother and toddler groups; check in your local YWCA or church or synagogue for information about when and where they meet.
□ There may be a family resource or mother's center in your area. These are usually set up and run by parents and are designed to meet the social and parenting education need of new mothers and fathers. To find out if there is one in your area, or how to start one, contact the Mother's Center Development Project (see Useful Addresses, p. 110) or contact the family service agency nearest you.
□ The LaLeche League runs breast-feeding support groups, which are really groups of mothers who meet on a regular basis. Find the chapter closest to you by checking the white pages of your phone directory or contacting the LaLeche League International (see Useful Addresses).

Week 18

Month: Dates:

MON

TUES

WED

THURS

FRI

SAT

SUN

Notes

WEANING FROM BREAST TO BOTTLE

Many mothers find the emotional rewards of breast-feeding increase as their baby gets older. Other mothers, however, feel that they have had enough by this stage and, once they start to introduce solid foods into the diet, feel that breast-feeding is less important. If you decide at around this age that you want to change to bottle-feeding, you must not feel guilty about stopping breast-feeding. You will have given your baby an excellent start.

The best way to stop is gradually. Replace one breast-feeding every other day or so with a bottle, so that your breast-milk gradually decreases and you do not feel too uncomfortable. Choose a feeding to drop where you seem to have less milk to begin with and one that the baby does not depend on too much for comfort – the bedtime feeding may be the last to go.

Some babies will reject the bottle at first: if so, continue to offer it at the same time over a period of days. Try leaving the baby longer so that she is more hungry. However, some babies become angry with this treatment and may turn against the bottle; try not to make it a battle between you. Other babies take to the bottle very readily and may even prefer bottle to breast, making weaning a quicker process than you antici-pated.

Games to play

Babies of this age need to put everything in their mouth if they are to understand what it is: it is therefore important to give the baby things to touch and hold which are safe and relatively clean, with no sharp edges. You don't have to sterilize toys, but it is a good idea to wash them regularly.

By playing with your baby in this way you are helping her to exercise muscles she cannot use unaided, as well as providing entertainment for her – and enjoyment for yourself at the same time.

Active play
By the time the baby is four to five months old, she is not only more robust but also very responsive. Many parents find physical play with babies of this age very rewarding as the baby obviously derives great pleasure from it.

There are several simple exercises which you can do with a baby of this age. Many babies enjoy standing on the floor and bouncing on their legs, testing out taking their weight, but they need to be held firmly while you bounce them. They will also like bouncing games on your knee. Most babies also enjoy being lifted up into the air and returned to safety.

Games and exercises for your baby
☐ Lie on your back on the floor with your knees raised and the baby sitting on your stomach, resting against your knees. Hold her hands and, as you sit up, lower her so that you are facing each other – then say "boo". Repeat, pulling her up as you lie down.
☐ Lie on your back and rest your baby on the lower part of your legs. Bring your knees up so that the baby "takes off" and lift her arms up into the air.
☐ Sit your baby facing you on your lap, and hold her hands. Say: "This is the way the lady rides, trit-trot, trit-trot, trit-trot" (jogging very gently). "This is the way the gentleman rides, a-gallop, a-gallop, a-gallop" (jogging with alternate legs). "This is the way the farmer rides, hobbledy-hoy, hobbledy-hoy" (uneven jiggling like a limping horse) "– and down into a ditch!" (dropping her gently).

☐ Bounce your baby on your knee to the tune and the words of "All around the mulberry bush the monkey chased the weasel, the monkey said it was all in fun, pop goes the weasel!"
☐ Finger games such as "Round and round the garden" and "This little piggy went to market" (see Week 12).
☐ Sit on the floor with your legs stretched out and the baby lying with her head towards your toes. Hold her hands and pull her up towards you as you lean back, and lower her as you rock forward, singing:
"Row, row, row your boat, Gently down the stream, Merrily, merrily, merrily, merrily, Life is but a dream."
Another song she might like is:
"I love to row in my big blue boat, My big blue boat, My big blue boat, I love to row in my big blue boat, Over the deep blue sea."

Week 19

Month: Dates:

MON

TUES

WED

THURS

FRI

SAT

SUN

Notes

CRYING AND COMFORTING

As your baby gets older you will realize the reason for his crying. He will generally cry from hunger only before established feeding times, or from tiredness at the times of day when he usually sleeps. You will know whether he is crying from frustration, or boredom, or because he wants you to pick him up. There should now be little unexplained crying; if your baby cries a lot more than usual you will have to assume that he is ill or is suffering from some discomfort such as teething.

However, your baby's pattern may change as he needs less sleep and he may cry when you put him down for his morning nap because he is not ready to sleep until a little later. There may also be times, especially when he is acquiring a new skill which uses a lot of energy, when he is more tired than usual and seems to need a little *more* sleep.

As he grows, he will need more stimulation and to be given new things to interest him and keep him happy; he may become bored if the toys and distractions he is given do not meet his new need to grasp, hold, and exercise his limbs. Remember that everyday objects are just as interesting as expensive toys at this stage.

Baby's meals

By the time your baby has become used to first solids on a spoon and perhaps had tastes of two or three different foods, you can start to build up these tastes into proper meals. It is best to proceed quite slowly, but to start giving the baby more at one particular meal – usually either lunch or dinner, whichever is most convenient for you. The best foods are still cereals and puréed fruits and vegetables, but you can try adding a little unsalted gravy or sieved meat. It is best to steer clear of eggs and cheese for a while yet because some babies are allergic to them or find them indigestible.

It's best to continue to introduce new foods one at a time so that you can be sure what it is if anything upsets your baby. Remember that his digestive system is still geared to a milk diet and that new foods may cause a slight upset at first. A baby won't be able to digest everything he's given; you will often notice that some food seems to pass through him almost undigested.

At this age you should certainly avoid giving your baby any convenience foods meant for adults, or any salt. A baby's kidneys are not mature enough for him to handle salt in any quantity, and this can damage them. Foods containing a lot of salt – or sugar – will also make your baby thirsty; if he then fills up with lots of juice or other drinks he may not have room for the milk that he needs. However, packages and jars of ready-prepared baby foods have their place and can be convenient (see below).

Save yourself time by cooking a little extra when preparing your own meals and putting it to one side for the baby; you would need to add salt or sugar to your meal later. You can also freeze small portions of baby food in yogurt containers or plastic ice trays in the freezer, or keep them for up to two days in the refrigerator.

It would be worth investing in a small hand blender or food mill at this stage; it will be in constant use for months.

Convenience baby foods

At this stage boxes or jars of ready-prepared baby foods may seem easier than the fuss of preparing your own meals. However, since many of these have the same bland taste and texture it is worth also getting your baby used to the taste of home-prepared foods. Always look carefully at the ingredients on boxes and jars. For example, you might want to avoid cow's milk products and find that a prepackaged meal contains large quantities of milk. Look for labels that indicate no added sugar on packages of biscuits and cereals as well as on jars of baby food. Several desserts contain sugar, and many convenience foods have added starch and protein. Home-prepared foods with no added starch or sugar are of most benefit for a plump baby.

Convenience foods have their place, however, and you shouldn't feel guilty about using them. On occasions it might be more valuable to spend half an hour playing with your baby and giving him your attention rather than leaving him to cry while you boil up and purée a few carrots or grate some meat.

Week 20

Month: Dates:

MON

TUES

WED

THURS

FRI

SAT

SUN

Notes

FEELING HER FEET

Up till now the baby may have been fascinated by her hands, both by watching them and putting them in her mouth. But around this time she may suddenly discover her feet and enjoy playing with them whenever she gets the opportunity, especially in the bath or while having her diaper changed. She will enjoy being on the floor on a rug with her feet uncovered.

At this age, she will like to stand upright, supported by you, and take her weight on her legs. At first she will probably bounce with both legs together, but then she will learn to hop and dance, taking the weight first on one foot and then another. If your baby loves this activity, which can be very tiring on your arms, she may enjoy a baby bouncer which can be suspended in a doorway, but wait until she can support her head well before using it. (Check first that your doorway has a suitable frame from which to suspend it.)

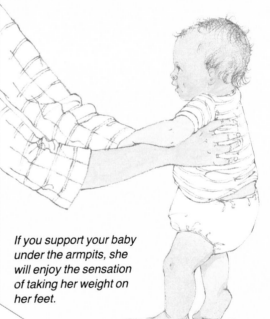

If you support your baby under the armpits, she will enjoy the sensation of taking her weight on her feet.

Diaper rash

Many mothers find that, once they start introducing their baby to a mixed diet, the baby's bowel movements change and in some cases diaper rash may result. Some babies become a little constipated when starting solids, while others have loose and frequent bowel movements. The baby's digestive system needs time to adjust to new foods and also the bacteria present in the baby's intestine tend to change when other substances are introduced. Mothers who have so far breast-fed their babies may find diaper rash becomes a problem when they introduce formula milk.

The most common form of diaper rash is caused by bacteria in the baby's bowel movements attacking substances in the baby's urine, to produce ammonia. This powerful alkali may smell very strong or even make your eyes water when you change the baby's diaper, and it will certainly inflame the baby's skin. If the skin gets sore and broken, it can be very difficult to cure, so prompt action is necessary as soon as the diaper rash starts to prevent it getting any worse.

Thrush is another cause of persistent diaper rash. This is a fungus which can also live in the baby's intestine and which causes a characteristic raised red rash, which may resist all treatment. It is possible to see the fungus as a white substance on the skin, but you may mistake it for zinc and castor oil cream or any other cream you are using to

ers. If you think this could be the cause, try changing the brand of disposable diapers or change your washing powder to a non-biological one. Some mothers find that diaper rash is less of a risk with cloth diapers or you can now buy ultra-dry types of disposables.

Preventing diaper rash
It helps to change the baby's diaper frequently, never leaving her for long in a wet or dirty diaper. If you can let her kick for a while without a diaper on, perhaps on a towel or a cloth diaper on a waterproof mat, that will also help. (The baby's skin can otherwise easily stick to a plastic mat, especially on hot days.) The bacteria which cause the problem do not survive well if exposed to air.

If leaving the baby without a diaper on makes too much mess, then try using a thin muslin diaper without plastic pants for a time, which will allow air to reach the skin. Always wash the baby's bottom well and dry it carefully when you change a diaper, to remove bacteria from her skin. Then apply a good barrier cream, such as zinc and castor oil, petroleum jelly or another diaper preparation cream.

Leaving the diaper off
It's a good idea to leave your baby to kick without a diaper at some changing times to allow the air to get to her skin. Remember not to leave her unattended on a raised changing mat – put the mat on the floor where you can watch her.

clear up the rash. If your baby has thrush, a doctor will prescribe a fungicidal cream.

Some babies have very sensitive skin and may be allergic either to the washing powder or fabric conditioner you are using, or to diaper softeners – or even to the substances used to perfume disposable diap-

Week 21

Month: _____ Dates: _____

MON

TUES

WED

THURS

FRI

SAT

SUN

Notes

ROUGH AND TUMBLE GAMES

Below are some ideas for more physical "games" for either fathers or energetic mothers to play with baby. Fathers can also give louder and rougher versions of "Pop goes the weasel" and "This is the way the lady rides..." (see Week 18). Some babies do not enjoy these rougher games, however, and find the sensation of being thrown in the air or suddenly "dropped" very alarming. If this is the case, find something gentler to play with your baby.

Airplanes Hold the baby under the arms and "fly" him around the room, swooping down and then up into the air.

Playing football Rest the baby on your knee, take his legs and mimic running with them, before pretending to kick a ball into a goal; you could give a running football commentary as you do it!

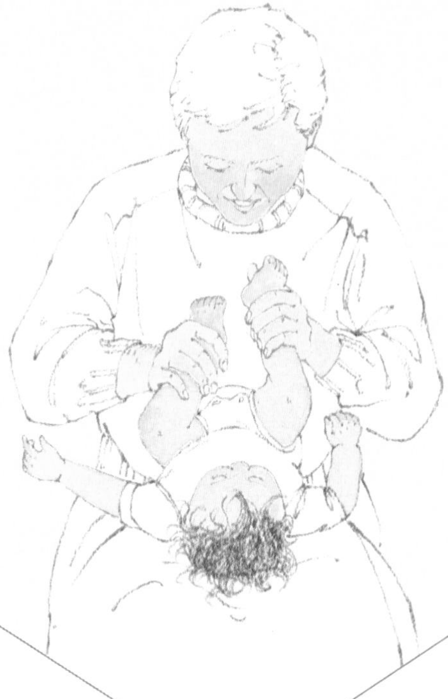

Fathers

At around this stage the baby may start to become more interesting to his father. Some fathers find tiny babies rather alarming, and do not feel confident in handling them. But as the baby becomes bigger and more robust, and begins to interact more with people, the father may, once the baby responds to him, discover he has a part to play.

At this same age many babies start to show an interest in familiar people other

A father's involvement
If your partner takes the baby out, or feeds him, from time to time, this will encourage the baby to think of his father as another loving person.

than their mother and to react to them as individuals. The particular characteristics of his father may be endlessly interesting for the baby – his more rugged features and his different voice. Many fathers play more "rough and tumble" games with their baby which they particularly enjoy – they may laugh with relief that this rather frightening person is only daddy after all.

Sharing the routine
Many parents find that it helps to build a strong relationship if the father develops a habit of doing something regularly with the baby. If your partner goes off to work early and the baby is an early riser, this can be a good time for father to get him up, perhaps amuse him while shaving or getting breakfast – and give you an extra half-hour in bed or some time to have a bath in peace.

Alternatively, the father may like to give his baby a bath at the end of the day. On the weekend, he might take the baby out shopping or for a walk, or could give him his lunch so that you get a break. Fathers can involve themselves with their baby in other everyday ways too, such as changing diapers and clothes, getting him ready to go out, making up feedings or giving the baby some of his solid food. This will help the baby to realize that food and comfort come from other people too.

This kind of support is all the more welcome when your partner doesn't wait to be asked to do things. It can be a great help to feel that the responsibility for the child is being understood and shared. A father who sometimes offers to take the baby off your hands, or who notices the baby needs changing before it has to be pointed out to him, will be taking away some of this pressure.

Building a bridge
It is important that every time the baby cries the father doesn't automatically hand him over to you. This would only reinforce the message that mother is the only source of comfort and will make it more difficult for the baby to form a relationship with, and trust, other adults. The father plays an important role in providing a bridge between the baby and his mother and the outside world – and the closer and more involved he is, the easier the baby's adjustment will be.

If you are thinking of returning to work in the near future, it is even more important for the father to involve himself in the baby's care. Not only can he help when you are not there, but the baby will be accustomed to being handled by someone other than his mother by the time the childcare arrangements begin.

See
Week 18
for Games
to Play

47

Week 22

MON

TUES

WED

THURS

FRI

SAT

SUN

Notes

LOOKING AFTER HER TEETH

When your baby has several teeth, you can start cleaning them. Do this by putting a little toothpaste on your finger and rubbing them gently. An older baby will enjoy chewing on a toothbrush but is unlikely to do any effective cleaning.

Help her to grow strong teeth by giving fluoride drops from birth – check with your dentist or doctor as to the level of fluoride in the local water supply and what dosage you should give. If you are regularly rubbing a fluoride toothpaste on her teeth, be careful not to let her swallow toothpaste as she could be getting too much fluoride.

The best way to ensure healthy teeth is to avoid giving your child too many sweet things, especially between meals. It is particularly important not to give her lots of sweet drinks in a bottle as the constant bathing of the teeth in sweet liquids can cause severe damage to growing teeth.

Teething

Babies vary considerably in the age at which they cut their teeth, though they will generally come through in the same order. Most babies cut their first teeth around five to seven months, though it is possible to have a first tooth as early as three months or as late as nine. Very rarely a baby is born with a tooth in place, and it is not uncommon for a baby to reach her first birthday without a single tooth having come through.

Teething is often blamed for many of the baby's troubles in the first year, including diarrhea, sickness, loss of appetite and a raised temperature, together with unexplained crying, night waking or general fretfulness. While teething may well cause some fretting, dribbling and frantic biting, it is unlikely to be the cause of more serious symptoms. If a baby is ill she should be taken to the doctor, and if she is crying or fretful you should look for some other cause such as boredom, thirst or perhaps the beginning of a cold or other illness, before automatically blaming teething.

Remember, too, that your baby dribbles not necessarily because she is teething but because she does not know how to swallow the saliva that is constantly being produced to clean and lubricate her mouth. At some time near the beginning of the second year she will learn to swallow this. Some babies dribble so much that their clothes are always wet, as are the sheets on their crib or carriage when you get them up from a sleep. If your baby dribbles a lot, you can use a bib while she is awake and put something absorbent under her head while she sleeps. It is dangerous to put a baby down for a sleep with a bib tied round her neck.

Teethers

If your baby appears in discomfort over teething, simply massaging her gums with your little finger may provide comfort. You can also help your teething baby by giving her hard things to bite or chew on, such as crusts or other hard foods like raw carrot. But never leave her alone with these because of the danger of choking.

Special teething rattles can be bought or teething devices with a gel inside them which can be cooled in the refrigerator: some babies get relief from the sensation of chewing or sucking something ice-cold. (Never use such a teething ring direct from the freezer as it will be so cold it could burn the baby's mouth.)

Teething gels, available at most pharmacies, can be rubbed on the baby's gums to anesthetize them slightly; provided you do not use them too often, they are unlikely to cause any harm. Don't get into the habit of regularly giving your baby acetaminophen syrup or other painkillers as these *can* be harmful in repeated doses.

See Week 10 for Baby's First Illness

See Week 48 for Healthy Teeth

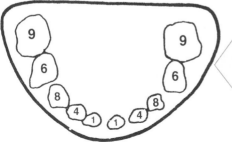

Order of teeth
The first teeth to come through are usually the front incisors, or the two middle teeth of the lower jaw, then the upper incisors. These are followed by the lower first molars and then the upper first molars at around twelve to fourteen months. The lower and upper canines – the sharp "eye teeth" – are cut at about eighteen months and the lower and upper second molars towards the end of the second year.

Week 23

Month: Dates:

MON

TUES

WED

THURS

FRI

SAT

SUN

Notes

Between four and five months your baby will have developed good control when reaching out and touching objects – he will be able to grasp them with one or both hands, although he will be clumsy in his attempts to pick things up.

He is learning to focus and will soon be able to assess the distance between his hand and a particular object and judge how far he has to reach. Instead of swiping at an object with a clenched fist, he will open his hands and wrap them around it.

He may bring the toy or object in his hand up to his mouth to explore it further, or at least nearer to his face so that he can study it more closely. He may try shaking it and, quite soon, will be able to feel it with both hands.

Objects which make a noise are particularly good for developing your baby's hand–eye coordination. He will learn that what he does with his hands can create a sound as well as making an object move where he wants it.

■ **DON'T FORGET** Once a day, if only for 15 minutes, do something just for you – go for a run, take a bubblebath, read a book, have a good chat on the phone with a friend.

Baby's changing diet

As your baby approaches six months he will be eating more solid food and cutting down on the amount of milk he needs in compensation. By now he may be eating three small meals a day and you can try cutting out the lunchtime breast- or bottle-feeding. Give water or diluted fruit juice instead – either in a bottle or in a trainer cup.

If you want your baby to eat a wide range of foods, it is important that you try to cut down on the amount of milk he drinks and offer a broad variety of foods to get him used to different tastes and textures. One way you can cut down on milk is by offering breast- or bottle-feeds *after* a meal – you should find he drinks less naturally. Some babies, however, seem to prefer sucking on breast or bottle to taking solid foods and you may have to go a little more slowly. But a baby who is taking five full bottles a day is not going to have room for solid foods – and if he does eat them he is likely to get fat.

Using a cup
Give your baby a trainer cup with milk or diluted juice in it. Even if he doesn't drink from it, give him an unbreakable cup with handles which he can play with in his highchair so that he gets used to the beaker at mealtimes. At first he will probably turn it upside down and use it as a teething device, or wave it around like a rattle, but eventually he will get the idea of what it is for.

Sample day's menu
Early morning Breast- or bottle-feeding.
Breakfast Cereal (porridge or sugar-free baby cereal) then breast- or bottle-feeding.
Lunch Puréed meat or fish and vegetables, or a jar meal, perhaps followed by puréed fruit.
Late afternoon Puréed fruit or mashed banana with cereal, followed by breast- or bottle-feeding. You could mix the fruit with natural yogurt once your baby is six months old.
Bedtime Breast- or bottle-feeding.

At this stage it is also important that your baby gets plenty to drink, as he will no longer be getting all the fluids he needs in his milk. Offer plain boiled and cooled water – though some babies, used to sweet breast-milk or formula, find this a bit of an insult. If so, use very dilute fruit juice – preferably unsweetened mixed with boiled water – and try giving it in a trainer cup. At first he will find the technique difficult to master but you can help by holding the cup and taking it away as soon as he shows signs of coughing or spluttering – or has had enough.

By six months your baby may be ready to take his meals in a highchair rather than on your lap. If you are breast-feeding, this will put a distance between the baby and your breast which may help you to drop a mealtime breastfeeding. Always stay with your baby – you will need to feed him at first and if he is chewing on a rusk or finger food you should be at hand in case he chokes or tries to climb out. Use a safety harness from the start when your baby is in the high-chair; if you introduce it only once he does try to get out, it may cause problems.

51

Week 24

Month: Dates:

MON

TUES

WED

THURS

FRI

SAT

SUN

Notes

LEARNING TO SIT

By about four months your baby will be able to sit with her head held up if you support her with your hands. By the age of six months she may be able to sit up by herself for a few seconds, but will need some support. Sit her on the floor propped up with cushions which will soften her landing when she flops.

Many babies can sit alone by about seven months, though they are very unsteady. Their backs will probably still be rounded and they will probably use their arms to support themselves.

At this stage it is rather unkind to sit your baby up surrounded by toys as the moment she lifts a hand off the ground to take a toy she is bound to fall over. Try sitting with her to give her support and encouragement.

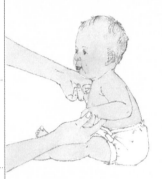

At first your baby's back will be very rounded and her head will pull her forward, so you will need to support her in a sitting position.

Once your baby can sit alone for short periods, you can support her with cushions. Cushions on the floor will prevent her from hurting herself when she falls over.

DON'T FORGET Your baby is due for her third DTP and third polio immunization.

Returning to work?

The decision of whether or not to return to work can be a hard one, especially if you have no obvious childcare arrangements. First you and your partner need to go carefully over your finances and see how much extra you will really be earning, after taking into account babysitting costs, travel to work and so on. Second, begin to look into suitable childcare arrangements. It is a good idea to ask other working mothers how they manage and what suits them best.

Choice of childcare

Very few offices provide on-site day care centers for the children of their employees. However, some employers offer a subsidy to employees who use nearby day care centers as a substitute for on-site care. If you are considering a day care center, you should consider only a licensed one. This will not necessarily guarantee the highest quality care for your child – each state has different licensing regulations – but it should mean that the center is directed by someone with a knowledge of early childhood education and that certain minimum health and safety standards are met. You will still need to evaluate carefully each center. Ask what the ratio of staff to babies is. Many experts feel there should be at least two qualified caregivers for every four to six babies. For information about both starting and evaluating early child care programs, contact The National Association for the Education of Young Children (see Useful Addresses, p. 110).

Another popular option for parents of very young children is a day care home. This is where someone, who may or may not have children of her own, cares for children in her home. The advantage of this arrangement can be that it provides a more homelike, family atmosphere. But in most states, there is no licensing method for these homes. The Department of Human Services in your county or state may be able to provide you with the names of reputable home day care providers in your area.

If you can't find a suitable day care situation outside the home, the other alternative

Making the decision

Most mothers feel guilty to some extent about leaving their child to go to work, and some may be conscious of the disapproval of either friends or relatives. It is worth thinking carefully about your own views and feelings. If you really think working isn't a good idea, you will probably find the guilt and stress very difficult to deal with, especially if other people put some kind of pressure on you too.

However, you may decide that you have to work for financial reasons, or you may feel that working enables you to afford some of the extras which make life easier, or that you need to have some time away from home and baby. If the childcare arrangements you make are suitable, there is no reason why you should feel guilty. Many mothers, particularly those who are able to work part-time, feel that they get more out of their children and enjoy the time they are together much more because they also have a break from them.

is to employ a nanny. Nannies can either live in or come to your home on a daily basis. They can be quite expensive, so if you have only one child you could think about splitting the cost with another working mother who has a baby about the same age as yours. Some nannies are trained, others simply have experience of working with children. Many are young, however, and may not want to spend a long time in one job, so you have to be prepared for frequent changes.

It is important to interview child caregivers or nannies carefully and to take up references. Make sure that you are happy with the way they are likely to look after your child. Make a list of things you consider important and ask their views – for example, on discipline and on what food your child should be given. Most of all be guided by your instinct – you will usually know whether the person is responsible, warm and caring. Let her handle your baby and see if you feel she would relate well to her.

Week 25

Month: _____ Dates: _____

MON

TUES

WED

THURS

FRI

SAT

SUN

Notes

SOCIAL BEHAVIOR

Your baby will now recognize other familiar faces as well as your own and may greet them with pleasure. But at around this time he may also begin to show fear of strange people, especially if they try to be too familiar, picking him up suddenly or making a fuss of him. Some babies show pronounced "stranger anxiety" by crying and appearing distressed if an unfamiliar person picks them up. Other babies are simply very shy and will bury their heads in their mother's shoulder when they see an unfamiliar face.

Babies of this age are unlikely to interact much with babies or other children they don't know well, though you may notice your baby plays quietly for longer if another baby is on the floor or in the playpen with him, and he may watch the antics of older children with pleasure as long as they are not too noisy and don't in any way threaten him.

DON'T FORGET Continue with your pelvic floor exercises (see Week 6).

Keeping fit

Looking after a baby is hard work, so it is important that you keep fit and healthy. You have had a lot taken out of you in the last year and if you are still feeling less fit than before you had the baby, or if you are overweight, start thinking about what you can do to change this.

Most crucial of all is your diet: make sure that you are eating well. If you are rushing around, you may not have time to fix proper meals for yourself but fill up on snacks instead; these may be fattening as well as not being very nutritious. Try to sit down at lunchtime when you feed your baby and eat something satisfying, even if it is only a simple meal like soup and a roll of whole-wheat bread, or a sandwich made with wholewheat bread, cheese, peanut butter or meat and salad. Eat fruit rather than cookies and take vitamin supplements if you

are not sure that you are eating well enough. You could increase your milk intake – if you don't like drinking milk, try taking it in another form such as yogurt.

If you can find the time, start doing some regular exercise. Try to turn your exercises into a game that you and the baby can play together – he may even be amused simply to watch you. If you find this hard on your own, join a local exercise class.

Swimming is excellent all-round exercise; some swimming pools have special sessions for mothers and babies and, if you go with a friend, one of you can mind the babies while the other gets some proper swimming done, even if it is only a couple of lengths of the main pool. Or you can go with your partner on weekends. If the pool is open in the evenings, you could possibly go on your own once a week.

◁ Stand or sit upright. Grasp your wrists with alternate hands, and lift both arms up until elbows, shoulders and wrists are level; hold this position. Grip really hard, and try to push your wrists towards your elbows. Push and relax several times, or until you begin to tire. This exercise is good for firming your breasts.

Lie face downwards on the floor with your forehead resting on your hands. Lift one leg behind you from the hip, keeping it straight. Lift it as high as you can, without bending the knee or turning your body. Lower it again and relax. Lift the other leg and relax. Continue the exercise several times or until you begin to tire. This exercise is good for your back. ▽

Lie on your back on the floor or bed, with arms outstretched and bent knees together. Keeping your feet and shoulders still, and twisting from your waist, swing both knees over to touch the floor or bed on the left, while your right hip points towards the ceiling. Then swing your knees over to the right, so your left hip turns towards the ceiling. Repeat several times. This exercise is good for your waistline. ▷

Week 26

Month: Dates:

MON

TUES

WED

THURS

FRI

SAT

SUN

Notes

SIX-MONTH MILESTONES

By six months your baby is likely to be eating three meals a day plus an extra bottle-feeding or an extra breast-feeding. She may want to feed herself by grabbing the spoon or picking up bits of food in her fingers.

She is probably able to sit for a few seconds on her own, or for longer propped up with cushions, and can roll from her stomach to her back and possibly vice versa. She may make crawling movements, though she is unlikely to make any real progress at this age.

She can reach accurately for objects within her reach and pick them up using her whole hand. She can also pick up an object with both hands, and will drop what she is holding if you offer something else.

Your baby will by now recognize a number of familiar faces and show particular pleasure in her mother and father. She may treat your body as if it is her own, poking fingers in your mouth and nose, while showing more respect for less familiar faces. She may well react with fear and alarm if you hand her over to a stranger.

Eating and sleeping

By the six-month stage your baby should have a fairly fixed routine of meals, nap times and bedtime. Up to now, she may have fitted in round your changing day, perhaps staying up late when friends came or you went out to family or friends in the evening, and having her meals juggled, with an extra breast- or bottle-feeding to fill in the gap. Now, however, it becomes more important to keep the baby to a regular routine if you are to avoid problems on both sides.

Most babies of this age will need two naps a day: one in the morning and one in the afternoon. The length of her naps will depend on how much sleep she needs overall and on the time she goes to bed in the evening. A wakeful baby may be up at six or seven o'clock in the morning, sleep for only half an hour in the morning and half an hour in the afternoon, and go to bed at eight or nine o'clock. Another baby might be up at seven or eight o'clock, sleep for an hour in the morning and two hours in the afternoon and

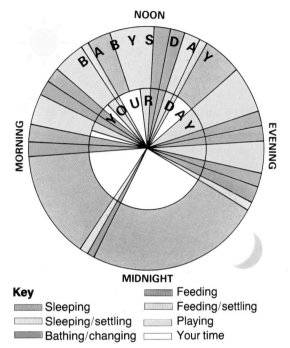

Key

Sleeping	Feeding
Sleeping/settling	Feeding/settling
Bathing/changing	Playing
	Your time

Breaking the night-waking habit

Your six-month-old baby may still be waking at night. If she is, and you are still giving a breast- or bottle-feeding at night, try to cut this out. The baby does not need the extra nourishment if she is eating well during the day, and giving her milk may stimulate her digestion, making sleep more difficult. Try offering water or diluted fruit juice in a training cup instead.

If you give your baby a lot of attention when she wakes, gradually give her less and less. Don't talk to her and don't put the light on; just check that all is well, offer a drink if you think she might be thirsty, then put her back in her crib and leave her. Let her cry a little, and if the crying persists go back and settle her again in the same way, until she goes back to sleep. Many parents steel themselves for a hard time and discover, to their surprise, that their baby settles down after very few nights, allowing the whole family to enjoy a good night's sleep.

still be ready for bed at seven in the evening.

If your baby is a wakeful one, try to extend her "nap" times by putting toys in the crib for her to play with on waking, or before she settles herself for a nap. Even if the baby doesn't sleep, it can refresh you both if she goes in her crib to play quietly while you get on with other things or put your feet up for twenty minutes or so. If she gets into the habit of playing in her crib at set times, she may accept this for quite a long period.

Mealtimes should be regular by now, and will fit around the baby's preferred nap times. For example, if your baby sleeps late in the morning, from 11.30 a.m.–1 p.m., she may not have her lunch until 1.30 p.m. and supper not until 6 p.m. Another baby might nap from 9.30–11 a.m. and be ready for lunch at midday; she may not be able to last later than 4.30 p.m. for supper and may then want something extra before going to bed.

If your baby wakes later, she may join the family in their breakfast, but an early riser may need her breakfast sooner, unless her early morning breast- or bottle-feeding will keep her going until you are ready to eat.

See Week 37 for Coping with Sleep Problems

57

Week 27

Month: _____ Dates: _____

MON

....

TUES

....

WED

....

THURS

....

FRI

....

SAT

....

SUN

....

Notes

■ PLAYING PEEKABOO

This becomes many babies' favorite game at this age and is one which can be infinitely adapted.

Cover your face with your hands and then take them away or peer round them. Or look up from a book, magazine or newspaper held between you and the baby (you might manage to read a few lines in between!).

The baby himself may discover he can hide behind something and become the active party in this game.

Equipping the older baby

Clothes

When buying clothes for a baby of six months you need to think more about how they will wash and wear, as crawling puts considerable stress on them. It is good for a baby learning to crawl, and beginning to stand and feel his feet, to go barefoot indoors when he can; socks may be necessary in cold weather, however, and you can get lined fabric booties with non-slip soles which will be useful for going out in the winter.

At this stage he may prefer trousers or overalls to all-in-one suits; when a baby starts to crawl his feet can work out of the toes of a suit and get caught up. Overalls are usually good value; if you buy a pair on the large side you can adjust the shoulder straps to make them shorter and turn up the trouser legs and they will last at least until the end of the first year. You can get overalls with snaps up the inside legs which makes diaper changing easier.

Jogging suits with separate tops and bottoms are also comfortable for a baby who is becoming mobile and will probably last longer than an all-in-one stretch suit. If you do buy a stretch suit, look for those which allow you to change diapers without having to take the whole garment off. Some have a flap in the back, others a zipper or snaps which go right down the leg.

Equipment

Your baby may now be outgrowing some "furniture" and needing new items. A bouncing chair, for example, becomes dangerous once the baby can sit forward and tip it up and he may be able to roll his Moses basket over or even try to climb out of the carriage if left to sleep in it unattended. This is the time to buy either a lowchair or highchair to feed your baby in; a highchair or one which converts is probably the best buy. Some models fold into a small chair and table for the toddler; others simply lift off a high stand to be used on the floor.

If your baby has outgrown the portable bassinet or Moses basket you might consider a portacrib for taking away with you or for when you want your baby to stay with friends or relatives for an afternoon or overnight. Portacribs come in many different shapes; you want one that your baby can still use once he can stand upright, so make sure the sides are high enough and that the base is firm.

A lightweight folding stroller will probably come into its own now; it is easy to take on public transportation, in the trunk of a car or on a plane. You may find it worth investing in an inexpensive, simple model if your carriage or stroller combination is heavy or takes up a lot of space when folded.

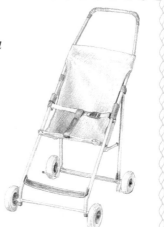

This highchair (far left) can be used with or without the tray and will later convert to a lowchair and table for an older baby.

A lowchair (left), which your baby may already have, is very useful for feeding; it comes with a separate stand and a tray.

A basic lightweight stroller (right) is both easy to fold and to transport.

Week 28

Month: _____ Dates: _____

MON

TUES

WED

THURS

FRI

SAT

SUN

Notes

▦ GRASPING AND HOLDING

By six months your baby will be able to reach out and grasp any object within her reach provided it is not too big or too small. She will seem to assess the size of each object before she touches it and may even appear to know how heavy it is. Some babies at around six months seem unable to touch any object without grasping it: your nose or hair may come in for some rough treatment!

If you offer her another object, she will drop the one she is already holding as she cannot concentrate on both. You may have to trick her into letting go of an object you do not want her to have by offering something else.

At this stage the more interesting things she has to touch and hold the better. Brightly colored rattles which make a noise are an obvious choice, but she will quickly get bored with the same ones. She will enjoy feeling for different shapes and for new textures other than plastic, so try to find different surfaces for her to explore. You can buy toys using textured materials or can make your own "feely board" by sticking on materials with different textural qualities such as corduroy, velvet, something fluffy and something slippery like silk.

Baby's day

thing that can be squeezed or squeaked. This can be an easy time for some mothers, when the baby is happy to sit and play with toys and other objects, while not yet being mobile enough to get into mischief.

Shopping

A baby of this age finds shopping trips entertaining on many different levels. A shopping mall holds many interests: she sees a variety of different people in the shops and loading up the purchases in a self-service store is great fun.

Even if it has taken a long time, you and your baby will probably have worked out some kind of routine by now, based around her sleep and mealtimes. However, you may want to vary things a little or there may be times of day when your baby seems bored or fretful and you don't really know what to do. The mothers of wakeful babies who do not sleep much may find it particularly hard to fill up the day with activities that amuse the baby while getting work done themselves.

It is a good idea to make one outing a day, whether to go shopping, to visit a friend or just for a walk. If you need to go shopping, choose a time of day when the baby has just slept so that you don't waste sleeping time by her dozing off in the stroller. There will be a lot for her to look at when you go out and you can help make shopping more enjoyable for her by giving her interesting things to do, like discarded packaging to play with or something to chew on.

Your baby will take an interest in all manner of new objects at this age. You can hand her something simple like a yogurt container and, provided she hasn't seen it before, she will inspect it carefully from all angles, turn it over in her hands, drop it and pick it up again. At this age she will find almost anything you have in the house (provided it is safe to give her) more interesting than the simple toys made for her age group. Try her with things like brushes, beads on a string, colored shiny paper, any-

Tips:

☐ Don't stick too rigidly to a routine. If the baby is irritable or hungry ahead of time, give her lunch or dinner, and perhaps take a little longer over the meal than usual by introducing some new finger foods for her to investigate, such as cubes of cheese, pieces of apple or bread and butter. If she seems tired, let her sleep early; you can plan an outing later on.

☐ If your baby seems bored, try doing something unexpected with her. Take her outdoors while you do some gardening – unless it's very cold you can even do this in the winter if you dress her in a snow suit; or put her in the backpack while you do some housework; or give her an extra bath at apparently the "wrong" time of day.

☐ There are some excellent daytime television programs for small children. If your baby is used to the television as background noise she may just ignore it, bit if she isn't, a children's program with songs and bright colors may hold her attention for a while.

☐ Babies love to watch other children, so an outing to the local playground or park where she can watch them may be fun. Or you can invite over a neighbor's child who may enjoy amusing the baby while her mother also gets a break.

Week 29

Month:　　　　　　　Dates:

MON

TUES

WED

THURS

FRI

SAT

SUN

Notes

LEAVING THE BABY

Get everything ready first, so that you can just pick up your bag and go with a cheerful wave. If your baby cries as soon as you hand him over, don't be tempted to keep taking him back and calming him. Just accept that his crying won't last long once you're out of sight.

It often helps to get everything ready the night before so that you are not rushing around looking for something vital when you're already late for work. Your baby too will find partings less distressing if this routine is always the same and there is a calm atmosphere in the mornings. If you can, try to get up that little bit earlier to allow you a short interlude just playing or chatting with your baby before leaving for work.

It might be best to choose your moment to leave when your baby is occupied with a toy or game. Although it won't work when he is older, it may not do any harm at this age if he doesn't see you go.

Leave phone numbers where you, your partner and the doctor can be contacted in an emergency.

DON'T FORGET Start thinking about ways you will need to baby-proof your home before your baby starts to crawl – safety covers on all electrical outlets, gates across stairways, no dangling electrical cords, etc. (see page 65).

Going back to work

You will probably have to decide sometime this year whether or not you will be returning to work. If your maternity leave is up and you decide to resume working, it may help to work a shorter week or leave early the first week or two. If you have had a trial day, when you left your baby in the care of the babysitter, nanny or whoever is caring for him, you shouldn't be too anxious about how he will react. Nonetheless, it is a wrench leaving your baby when you first go back to work. Console yourself with the thought that he is probably much happier about it than you are.

Many working mothers do feel guilty about leaving their babies. All the research that has been carried out, though, shows that babies left with suitable, caring mother substitutes do not suffer. The children remain more attached to their parents than the nanny or babysitter and show no harmful effects, even if the mother works full-time. Some children of working mothers seem more secure and less clingy than those who have never or hardly ever been out of their mother's company.

You will inevitably find your double job very tiring at first, especially as you settle into a new routine. An important consideration is to plan ahead so that the week's shopping is done, the house does not end up in total chaos and you have some time for yourself as well as for your baby and your partner. Your partner should be able to help you with some aspects of running the home as well as sharing childcare (see below). Don't expect too much of yourself, especially at the beginning; life will improve as you all adjust to the new routine.

It is also important that you sort out the arrangements you will make when your child is ill, as he inevitably will be. A nanny could probably cope with a baby who is sick but babysitters who look after other children too would be unable to. If your employer is sympathetic, this should not be too much of a problem, but if he or she is not, or if your child is ill a lot, you may have to think of other arrangements.

Perhaps your partner will agree to sometimes take time off when the baby is ill or when the babysitter or nanny is unable to work; otherwise you might end up with a situation where you have taken all your holiday allowance and your partner still has most of his left, which is not going to suit anybody.

Mixed emotions

On your first days back at work, you may feel a mixture of emotions: relief at having made all the necessary arrangements, and satisfaction in having time to think about something else or to get on with a task without constant interruptions, but at the same time worry about how the baby is doing without you.

If you find you are missing your baby constantly while you are at work, or feel very emotional all the time, you may be wondering whether you were right to return to work. It is best not to make a sudden decision to give up work until you've been back a few weeks and have settled into it, as you may otherwise regret the decision. If you continue to feel this way, however, you may decide that the money you earn is not worth all the anxiety.

Organizing your day

It can help to sort out certain daily tasks in advance with your partner; one of you gets the baby dressed while the other gets breakfast, and you perhaps take it in turns to take the baby to the babysitter or day-care center. Work out who will get any shopping needed.

Before you return to work, if possible, make yourself have a trial week when you get yourself and the baby up, have breakfast and get out of the house and to the day-care center or babysitter on time. This will lessen your anxiety on the big day and being left with the sitter for short periods will help both baby and babysitter to adjust.

Week 30

Month: Dates:

MON

TUES

WED

THURS

FRI

SAT

SUN

Notes

BABY'S PERCEPTION

If your baby drops something, she will start looking down to see where it has fallen. Instead of a dropped object "disappearing", she will now realize that it is still there, but in a different place. At this stage she may infuriate you by repeatedly dropping things out of her carriage, crib or highchair. It is important to understand that this is part of her development, and if you hand things back as part of a game, you will delight her.

You can make the game even more interesting when your baby is in the highchair by putting something on the floor – such as a metal tray – which will make a loud noise when objects are dropped on to it from a height. Give your baby a good supply of unbreakable items and encourage her to drop them to entertain herself while you are getting her lunch.

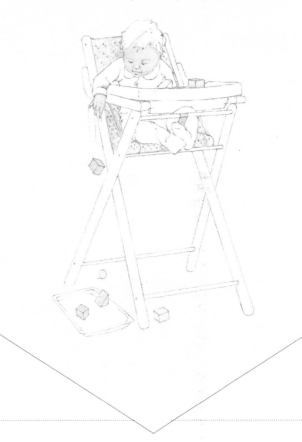

DON'T FORGET Simple household objects that your baby can handle safely, like wooden spoons or large keys, will be as interesting to your baby as elaborate toys.

Safety and the mobile baby

Although only a minority of children will be crawling properly at this age, many babies will be able to move around in one way or another. Some manage to shuffle backwards and forwards very slowly and others learn to roll over and over. However, your baby will soon learn to move – perhaps when least expected – and you should not rely on being able to put her down and go out of the room, safe in the knowledge that she will still be in the same place when you come back. Now is the time to think about making the home safer for a mobile baby. Some of the precautions may seem premature, but remember that you will not know what your baby is capable of doing until she does it.

Make sure all dangerous objects are out of reach and similarly any small breakable objects which might cut her. Fires should be screened with a fireguard, screwed into the wall. Any bookshelves or tables which are unstable should be fixed in some way so that the baby cannot overturn them by bumping into them or trying to pull herself up. If you have doors with glass panels, think about putting in safety glass. Children have been seriously cut and injured by breaking glass doors. (Safety film is illegal as a permanent glass door replacement.) Keep ashtrays or poisonous materials such as bleach or paint stripper out of reach. If you have kitchen or bathroom cupboards at floor level, fit safety catches to the doors.

You will also at this stage need to use a safety harness in the baby's stroller or highchair, to stop her trying to wriggle out.

Steps and stairs

If you have steps in the house – perhaps a couple of steps leading down into the kitchen – it can help to put a soft mat or rug at the bottom of them in case she falls down. Alternatively you could fit a stairgate; make sure it is properly fixed, and don't be tempted to keep climbing over it, especially when you are carrying the baby, as this can be dangerous. If the steps are in a place where you are coming and going all the time, it may be safer to do without a gate and make the area safe in other ways. Once your crawling baby learns to climb stairs, though, a stairgate is probably essential.

Week 31

Month: Dates:

MON

TUES

WED

THURS

FRI

SAT

SUN

Notes

WHAT TO TAKE ON A VACATION

Pack a travel bag for baby and keep it handy. Put in it: diapers, baby wipes, a change of clothes, the baby's food and drink, one or two favorite toys and, if appropriate, something to nibble or chew on.

If you are going abroad on your vacation, check on the local availability of certain goods, for example baby formula and disposable diapers, so you don't have to take two weeks' supply with you.

Take a first aid pack containing infant acetaminophen syrup, sun protection cream with a high sun block factor, ointment for insect bites or cuts, cream for diaper rash. You may be able to get medicine to counter diarrhea with a doctor's prescription.

You may also need to sterilize feeding equipment and you could consider taking a gadget for boiling water. (You will need to bring an electrical adapter to work appliances on a foreign electricity circuit.)

Whenever you go out with your baby you will need to take the essentials with you: change of diapers, food and drink, your baby's "cuddly". Baby wipes are convenient for changing diapers in an awkward spot.

Traveling with baby

At some point in your baby's first year you are likely to have a family vacation or to make a long journey to visit relatives or friends. Traveling with a baby can be difficult, especially once he has become mobile and wants to explore everything. However, if you plan your journey with care it should not be too difficult, whether you are traveling by car, train or plane. Always pack a separate bag containing everything you need for the baby (see opposite).

Air travel is probably the most difficult with a young child, as there is little room to change diapers and nowhere for him to crawl or sit (except your lap). You can, however, book a sky-crib on some long flights – ask when you make your booking. You will then usually be seated in the most comfortable part of the aircraft, where there is room for the sky-crib to be attached and thus more leg room. Give the baby a drink or breast-feed him at take-off and landing to prevent the pressure building up in his ears and causing pain; this is particularly important if he has a cold or catarrh.

If you are traveling by car, try to time your journey to fit in with your baby's nap and mealtimes to make the journey easier for everyone. You can buy a plastic tray which fits on to some car safety seats, enabling you to give the baby something to eat and toys to play with. Break your journey frequently to give a mobile baby a chance to let off steam. Always stop for a while if he is irritable; few people can really concentrate on driving with a screaming baby in the back of the car.

Make provision for unforeseen disasters such as a breakdown or traffic jam and have extra food and drink in the car. If it is winter, have warm clothes in case you break down miles from anywhere.

A backpack is an excellent way of transporting the baby on foot, especially across fields or uneven paths.

Keeping baby amused
In the car
- [ ] Play "Peekaboo" over the front car seat.
- [ ] Keep a supply of interesting objects in the front to hand the baby when he gets bored.
- [ ] Hang a toy which the baby can operate from the coat hook or roof of the car.
- [ ] Sing songs, clap hands or play a musical tape.

On a train
- [ ] Walk up and down the corridor and look out of the windows.
- [ ] Play "Pat-a-cake" and other games on your knee.
- [ ] Some trains have small fold-down tables you can use as a play-tray or a lunch table, if the people in the seats opposite don't mind.
- [ ] If your baby is getting irritable, hold him firmly and soothe him – the noise and movement of the train may lull him to sleep.

On a plane
- [ ] Walk the baby up and down when they are not serving drinks or lunch.
- [ ] Play bouncing games on your knee.
- [ ] If you have seats with leg room at the front, put down a mat and some toys and let the baby play there.
- [ ] Keep one or two new and interesting toys on a long journey for when he's bored with everything else and you are feeling weary.

See Week 18 for Games to Play

See Week 42 for Family Vacations

See Week 46 for Safety and First Aid

Week 32

Month: Dates:

MON

TUES

WED

THURS

FRI

SAT

SUN

Notes

■ BATHING THE OLDER BABY

Once your baby has been sitting without support for some time, she will probably want to sit up in the bath and play with her toys. Brightly colored boats and ducks are fun, but probably best of all are containers which can pour, fill and empty. Stacking cups, some of which have holes in the bottom, are ideal, or you can use empty plastic bottles or containers of different shapes and sizes.

To make bathtime safer, put a rubber non-slip mat in the big bath or buy a support to help a newly sitting baby stay upright. Never leave a baby unattended in the bath in case she slips or falls.

It may still be safer and more economical to use the baby bath at this stage. You can put it inside the big bath to get your baby used to that environment and so that it doesn't matter if there is a lot of splashing. Or put her in the adult bath with a rubber safety mat.

Developing skills

Children are individuals and as such develop at their own pace and in their own way. Your pediatrician or family doctor will, in all likelihood, perform periodic screenings of your child's development. These are normally done in conjunction with routine checkups.

Many things are taken into account when considering a child's development: his movement, co-ordination, physical growth, speech and understanding of speech, hearing, vision, and emotional and social awareness. There are also certain well-recognized developmental "landmarks" – mental and physical skills which children acquire in much the same way. For example, if your baby does not raise his head and shoulders from a face-down position at 4 to 6 months or say simple two-syllable worlds, like "Mama" and "Dada", at 8 months, this could indicate developmental delay. If your child's development is lagging in any area, your doctor will closely monitor it or he or you may want to have a more comprehensive assessment done at a university hospital or clinic.

Remember that babies' skills develop at very different rates and in different ways – some babies crawl as early as 5 months and others not until late in the first year; some learn to use their hands more quickly than others. But if you are concerned about any aspect of your child's growth, don't hesitate to speak with your doctor about it or seek an evaluation from a specialist. In some states, developmental screenings are available free of charge for pre-school age children through

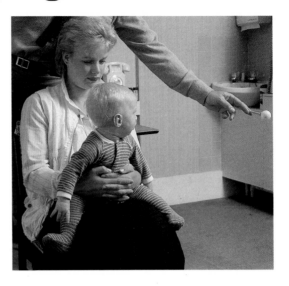

the school district. Some areas also have early intervention programs which offer screenings for children from birth up to the age of three.

Hearing and vision screening

Hearing and vision problems can interfere with your child's development. For example, normal speech development depends on the ability to hear well. For this reason, all children should have hearing and vision tests at regular intervals during early childhood. The American Medical Association recommends that ideally, children should have hearing screenings at 8 to 9 months, at 3 years and at 5 years. In the preschool years, preliminary hearing and vision tests are carried out by your family physician or pediatrician during routine visits. If these tests give your doctor reason to suspect that your child has a vision or hearing impairment, he will refer you to a specialist, who will conduct further tests on your child.

Responding to sounds
You may start to notice that your baby jumps or looks round at a sudden noise. She may also look up if you make a sound she associates either with food – perhaps a spoon scraping a dish or the kettle boiling – or with some other pleasurable event, such as daddy opening the front door. If she is showing these kind of responses at home but doesn't respond to the doctor's testing, ask for another test.

See Week 7 for well-baby examinations

Week 33

Month: Dates:

MON

TUES

WED

THURS

FRI

SAT

SUN

Notes

FINGER FOODS

Many babies enjoy finger foods which they can pick up and eat themselves. Try giving different foods in this form, such as the ideas below. Babies of this age may like small items such as peas which they can eat one at a time when they have mastered the pincer grip (see Week 36). Use pie cutters to make more interesting shapes from cheese, bread or cooked potato.

Cubes of soft cheese
Slices of hard-boiled egg
Cooked pasta shapes
Toast or bread fingers with soft cheese or smooth peanut butter
Hamburgers cut into cubes
Chunks of fish off the bone

Sliced fruit e.g. banana, pear, kiwi fruit
Tomato slices (without skin)
Mashed or baked potato cut into shapes
Pieces of soft vegetable e.g. avocado, cooked carrot or beans
Raw carrot slices

Feeding the older baby

two spoons, one for the baby and one for you, you can scoop up food which misses his mouth and pop it in, and you can also feed him if he gets too frustrated. Some babies like to get hold of the food in their fingers and simply play with it. It is important that you let them do this, at least from time to time, preferably at the end of a meal. It won't take long to wipe down the baby and the highchair when he has finished.

Feeding himself
Many babies want to feed themselves at this stage. This is very messy, but do encourage it, because it will help his co-ordination and this freedom will make mealtimes happier for him.

Whenever possible, sit down and eat with your baby. He may enjoy tasting a mouthful or two of your meal and may offer you some of his. Eating together will help him think that mealtimes are fun. When he indicates that he has had enough and turns his head away, don't force food on him or he may start resisting all solid food.

By this stage your baby will probably be getting much of his nourishment from solid food and milk will have become an additional drink rather than a basic, although it remains an excellent source of protein and vitamins. If your baby is slower in switching over to solids and still prefers milk, don't worry; at this age he can do perfectly well on breast- and formula milk provided he gets some solid food as well, particularly containing iron. If you want to wean your baby off milk, though, try offering it in a cup rather than a bottle and only give it after, not between, meals.

Provided the baby's diet is balanced overall, you need not feel that every meal has to be perfectly balanced in itself. It is quite all right to have just protein at one meal, or just bread, or potato and vegetables, at another. Your baby will now probably be ready for lumpier foods and thicker textures.

Feeding himself allows the baby to eat as much as he wants as quickly as he wants, which will help to avoid mealtime problems later. Put newspaper down on the floor under the highchair, put a large bib on your baby and let him get on with it. If you have

Mealtime ideas
Baked custard
2 cups of milk, 2 eggs, 1 tbsp clear honey or brown sugar.

Beat the eggs, add milk and honey or sugar and put the mixture in an ovenproof dish. Stand it in a tray of hot water and bake in the oven at 325°F for an hour or until set.

Milk puddings are easy to make and a valuable source of protein. Beware of instant puddings as many of them are mostly starch and coloring.
Hamburgers
4oz minced beef, half a small onion (finely chopped), scoop of tomato purée, 1 egg, plus 1 egg yolk

Mix the ingredients together, roll into flat shapes and grill or fry with very little oil or butter. Chop up before serving.

See
Week 40
for Weaning
to a Cup

Week 34

MON

TUES

WED

THURS

FRI

SAT

SUN

Notes

▪ LEARNING TO CRAWL

Babies are very varied in the age at which they learn to crawl. Some crawl as early as five or six months, others never learn to crawl at all but go straight from sitting and perhaps bottom-shuffling to walking.

Learning to crawl can be a frustrating process for some babies. They may be able to get up on hands and knees but then rock, unable to make any progress, and fall down on their faces. Others may try to pull themselves along with their arms but then end up shuffling backwards.

Some babies learn to crawl on their stomachs before they learn to get up on their hands and knees. A few crawl on hands and feet like a bear. Other babies who cannot actually crawl get around well by a combination of rolling over, shuffling and "creeping" backwards.

Your baby may take all her weight on her arms and legs but still be unable to move forward. Eventually she will master the technique – much to her delight.

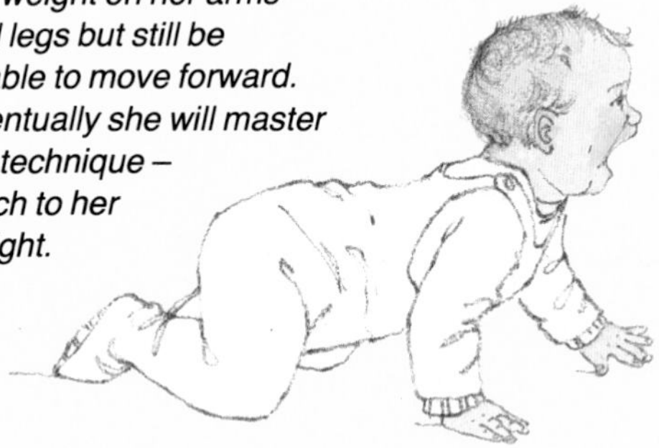

Toys for the older baby

At around eight months your baby will be developing fast. She needs to handle as many different objects as possible to find out what they do. Until recently, her main use for toys or any objects within reach was to put them in her mouth. Now she is beginning to experiment and explore what can be done with them. She will bang things, shake them, pull them and stroke them.

She is also beginning to understand how things work once it has been demonstrated. If you press a button and a toy squeaks, she will try to press it too. If you are writing with a pen, she may grab the pen and try to "write" as well as trying to put it in her mouth. She may become interested in toys with movable parts or those which come apart. She will enjoy handling things with different textures and others which make a noise.

A baby of this age can be happy on the floor or in her playpen for quite long perods provided she has enough to amuse her. Besides toys, you can give her things like cardboard boxes, containers of all kinds, old magazines to scrumple, tear and chew, aluminum foil pans which make a noise when banged or scrunched, saucepans and wooden spoons, and scraps of material. Toys designed for older children, provided they are safe, have great appeal for many babies (cars with wheels that go round and doors that open, for example). If she is playing with anything that could be dangerous if broken, keep a watchful eye on her.

Once your baby enjoys looking at brightly colored pictures and likes opening and shutting things, this may be the time to buy a few simple board books of different sizes or shapes. A small thick book, a large flat one and another which folds out will keep a baby of this age busy. Board books are also good for a teething baby to chew on. You can also get plastic books which go in the bath, and rag books which can be washed when they get grubby.

Baby walkers
There is some debate about whether baby walkers help your baby to walk, but there is no doubt that some babies love them. If you are considering buying one, it might be worth trying one out at a friend's house first to see if your baby likes it. Choose one which is stable and comfortable, and which meets government safety requirements.

Babies who are frustrated by their inability to crawl at this stage may get a sense of achievement from moving around in a baby walker. However, only let the baby use the walker for short periods or she will miss out on important floor play and learning to balance, sit and crawl.

Never leave a baby unattended in a walker and always use it on a flat, unrestricted floor, with a clear path away from fires, ungated steps or other dangers.

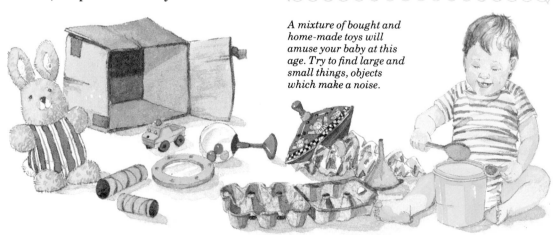

A mixture of bought and home-made toys will amuse your baby at this age. Try to find large and small things, objects which make a noise.

Week 35

Month: Dates:

MON

TUES

WED

THURS

FRI

SAT

SUN

Notes

THE DOCTOR'S EXAMINATION

Help the doctor to examine your baby by holding him gently but firmly on your lap. When visiting the doctor, remember to dress him in clothes which will come off easily, either for an examination of the chest or if he needs an injection.

For a throat examination, cradle the baby's head in your arm and hold his hands down so that he cannot try to push the doctor's hands away. Talk reassuringly.

Chest examination
Sit the baby upright on your lap and remove the clothes covering his chest. Be ready to turn the baby round so that the doctor can listen to both front and back.

Ear examination
Hold the baby's head firmly against your chest with one hand, and with the other hold down his free hand. Then turn him round for the other ear to be checked.

Common illnesses

Babies and small children are likely to catch colds and other minor illnesses simply because they have built up little resistance to them, having not been exposed to them before. While a baby is breast-fed, the mother passes on her immunity to a range of illnesses, but this gradually wears off after the baby is weaned. So often towards the end of the first year, and throughout his second year, your baby may well get ill with something other than a cold for the first time.

It is not unusual for babies to run quite a high temperature in cases where an adult's would hardly be raised at all. Many young children have a high temperature at the beginning of an ordinary cold, and a baby with an illness such as German measles or roseola can run very high fevers. If your baby has a raised temperature, keep him cool – take blankets off his crib, for example, and if he is really hot sponge him down with cool water. Acetaminophen syrup will bring down a temperature as well as relieving pain. If the temperature stays high, consult your doctor.

Coughs and colds sometimes lead to other infections of the throat, ear or lungs, because thick mucus provides an ideal breeding ground for bacteria. A secondary infection may result in another sudden rise in temperature after the baby had seemed much better. A baby with a sore throat will not only be restless and in pain but may refuse food or drink, or may be sick. An ear infection can cause severe pain and the baby may tug or pull his ear.

Bronchitis and pneumonia are lung infections which can occasionally follow a cold or, more frequently, occur after a childhood disease such as measles or whooping cough. The symptoms are usually a bad cough, shortness of breath and a temperature. Your baby will need to see a doctor.

Childhood diseases
Measles, chicken pox, mumps, German measles, roseola and whooping cough are the most common childhood diseases. You can protect your baby against whooping cough from three months and against measles at around fifteen months. A new vaccine is now available for mumps and German measles (rubella), to be given with the measles vaccine.

German measles and roseola are usually mild, especially in young babies. They rarely last long and need no special

Giving medicine
Many medicines are extremely sweet and most babies will like taking them; offer medicine from a spoon, or a specially designed, non-spill tube, with the baby sitting on your lap or in the high-chair. If he really hates the medicine, or feels too ill to take anything, try using a clean dropper to squirt the medicine into the back of the mouth so that he has to swallow it. (Ask your doctor for the best way to give medicine to a child who resists it.)

treatment. Chicken pox can be either very mild or quite severe and you should try to prevent your baby scratching or the spots can become infected. Measles can take quite a severe form and is sometimes followed by ear or lung infections, so the baby should be nursed carefully. Always see your doctor to confirm that your child has any of these illnesses; he or she can help make the correct diagnosis and offer advice.

Nursing your child
If your baby is ill, you will have to drop everything else and dedicate yourself to looking after him. Many ill babies require a great deal of comforting and may need to be carried around all the time. A baby with a fever will often be very drowsy but sleep only for short periods before waking and crying again; it may help to lie down on the bed with him, so that when he wakes he is comforted by seeing you there.

Offer frequent drinks of water or diluted juice; your baby may not take much at a time. Offer food if he will take it, but don't press food on an ill baby who doesn't want it; this may make him sick. Some babies with a temperature produce very strong urine which stings them, and others may have diarrhea, so change diapers frequently and use a protective cream to prevent diaper rash.

An ill baby usually means broken nights, so go to bed early yourself and get as much rest as you can. You could sleep in a spare bed next to the crib to reassure the baby if he wakes.

See
Week 10
for Baby's
First
Illness

See
Week 8
for First
Immunizations

Week 36

Month: Dates:

MON

TUES

WED

THURS

FRI

SAT

SUN

Notes

■ MANUAL DEXTERITY

Up to now your baby has only been able to take hold of objects by scooping with her whole hand and picking them up in her palm. From now on, however, she will learn to poke at things with one finger and to pick up small objects between forefinger and thumb, in 'the pincer grip'. Once your baby has acquired this skill, she will love anything that she can pick up in this way. Give her small bits of food to eat like peas, crumbs of bread or grains of cereal.

The mobile baby may crawl around the room picking up all the tiny bits of fluff or dirt she can find on the floor or carpet. These too will go straight into her mouth, so it is important to keep the floor clean. Make sure also that there are no small toys, parts of toys or other objects left on the floor which could cause her to choke, such as pins, buttons, small wheels off toy cars or tiny pieces of Lego.

The clinging baby

they are left with someone they know and in a familiar environment. A baby left in the care of a familiar figure with plenty to amuse her, and whose daily routine is followed, is unlikely to be unhappy for long.

Saying goodbye
If you have to go out, you will find it easier if you get everything ready beforehand so that you can leave at once. A prolonged leave-taking is likely to make things much worse for both of you.

At around this age many babies develop what is known as separation anxiety. They become very clingy and cry every time you put them down, pop out of the room, or go out of sight. A mobile baby may crawl around after you wherever you go and a baby who cannot crawl may cry piteously when you move away. Even a baby who has been quite happy to stay with a known person, or to play on her own for a while, may suddenly hate being left by you even for short periods. A baby who becomes very anxious may continue to want her mother constantly with her until some time well into the second year.

For mothers who have just settled back into a working routine, it can be an extra source of stress when their baby reaches this stage and starts to protest violently when she leaves for work. While it is distressing to leave a baby who is crying for your return, be reassured that the tears will quickly stop once you are out of sight and that the baby forgets much sooner than you will!

Sometimes babies continue to show great anxiety every time you leave them because they sense that you yourself are nervous about leaving them. This is only reinforced if you change your mind and decide not to leave her after all because she is crying. It is important to realize that almost all babies cry on separation from their mothers but that this is usually short-lived, and won't do her any harm. Babies protest much less if

If you are at home with your baby, you may find it hard that she still clings to you and cries whenever you step inside the bathroom or outside the back door. Almost the only thing you can do about this phase is to accept it and to take her with you as much as possible.

Around this age is probably a bad time to choose to go away and leave your baby with a relative or friends. If you wait till this phase is over, she will accept being left much more readily.

Making it easier
If your baby is clingy, get her used to spending short periods with another known person, perhaps her father, a grandparent, or a friend she sees often. You could have the friend's baby one morning a week in return. Once she begins to accept that you sometimes leave and that you *do* return, this will stand you in good stead if you ever have to leave her for a while unexpectedly.

When you leave her, do so quickly and cheerfully to show there is nothing to worry about and that crying won't make you change your mind.

If your baby likes to be carried and you have to put her down to get on with household tasks, try to turn them into a game for her. Play "peekaboo" while you are washing, or tickle her in the middle of the dusting. Handle and talk to her as you work, to show that you're not ignoring her.

See Week 14 for Leaving Baby at Home

See Week 29 for Going Back to Work

Week 37

Month: _____ *Dates:* _____

MON

TUES

WED

THURS

FRI

SAT

SUN

Notes

HAND COORDINATION

By this age your baby will be able to use both his hands together. Instead of discarding one object when handed a second, he may hold them both and compare them. He may play with them together, banging them, putting them down together and then picking them up again. He is learning to let go of things in a controlled way by unclenching his fingers.

He will also be able to pass an object from one hand to another, and to test whether one fits inside another. His movements have become less haphazard and are more coordinated as he acquires greater control of his fingers. He will soon be able to wave from the wrist, and point with just his forefinger, rather than making all such movements with his whole arm.

Your baby will be interested in seeing whether one object will fit inside another and will spend a lot of time working out what fits where.

He may learn to point at things he wants and to hold up his arms if he wants you to pick him up.

Coping with sleep problems

Whether your baby has never slept through the night, or has slept well from an early age, sleep problems can develop around this stage. These may occur even in a formerly good sleeper because of his anxiety at being separated from you. A habit of waking in the night may develop after an illness, during which your baby woke frequently and was nursed by you or taken into your bed. Even a baby who is very tired at bedtime can now resist sleep. He may protest loudly at being put down and continue to cry for long periods.

Time for bed
If you are friendly but firm at bedtime, and follow a consistent routine, your baby will eventually realize that this is the time for sleeping.

Early wakers

If your baby wakes early in the morning, you may be able to keep him amused by putting toys and interesting objects in or near his crib. A musical toy or an activity center which he can operate himself are very good for this purpose. Some babies, however, seem to want attention from the moment they wake. Taking him into your bed may please him and give you a rest.

You could try shifting his bedtime to a slightly later time, by half an hour or so, to give you a little longer in the mornings. This usually works if you are persistent – bear in mind that for the first few days he is likely to wake at the usual time anyway. If your baby wakes very early and then goes back for a nap quite early in the morning – say waking at 5.30 a.m. and then napping for an hour or more at 9 a.m. – it may be worth delaying his nap time too, to help him realize he needs a little more sleep in the morning. Again, this won't show results for the first few days and you may have an irritable baby on your hands for a time, but it should work if you persist.

The bedtime routine

It is necessary to sort out a consistent way of dealing with this phase, to reassure your baby that there is nothing to be afraid of and that you have not deserted him – but that it is bedtime. It may help to really define the bedtime routine you follow at this time.

Take time over his supper, play a quick game or two with him before his bath. You could sing a lullaby as you get him ready for bed to put him in a calm frame of mind. Put on his diaper and night clothes in the same place, then carry him to his crib. If you have a mobile, perhaps look at that together, then give him a cuddle and his bottle- or breast-feeding – and put him to bed. If he cries, give him a few minutes to settle, then go back and rub his back or stroke his hair – but don't pick him up again. Keep going back at regular intervals till he goes to sleep.

If your baby wakes frequently in the night, try the same technique. Go in briefly to let him know that you are there, and check that there is nothing wrong, then leave him. If he continues to cry, go back to check every so often, perhaps leaving it a little longer each time. Remember that you need your sleep and it won't hurt him to cry a little, as long as he knows you are there and will come if he really needs you.

See
Week 26
for Eating
and Sleeping

Week 38

Month: _____   Dates: _____

MON

TUES

WED

THURS

FRI

SAT

SUN

Notes

SAFETY AT HOME

Your baby will soon develop new skills such as pulling himself up to a standing position and climbing up on the stairs and furniture. Make sure that you anticipate this stage by putting dangerous objects out of reach and fixing any furniture which might topple over. Use a stairgate on the stairs. Cover electrical sockets with childproof safety covers and fix safety catches to cupboard doors and drawers within his reach. You can even buy a safety catch for the refrigerator if your baby continually tries to open it.

Now that your baby is more mobile it is even more important to make sure that he is strapped into his high-chair or stroller, especially if you leave him for a moment. It is worth strapping very active babies into a supermarket cart too. Never be tempted not to strap a baby into his car seat, no matter how violent his protest.

Time to yourself

As your baby gets older you may begin to feel that you have far too little time for yourself or for your partner. At the end of a day, after the baby is in bed and the meal has been cooked and eaten, the toys tidied away and chores like ironing done, you may want to do nothing else but go to bed. If you are working as well, there will seem even less time to devote to yourself.

It is important that you feel happy and fulfilled – otherwise you cannot enjoy your baby or your relationship with your partner. It is worth setting aside a special time each week which you spend with your partner, uncluttered by domestic chores. Perhaps you could also arrange to have one evening a week off by yourself, to visit friends or perhaps to go to an evening class. Your partner might also like an evening to go out with friends or play some sport. If you have agreed on this in advance and you both have your own time, you will not resent the fact that one of you seems to go out more than the other.

It is worth establishing some kind of regular evening babysitting arrangement, either with a relative, with a neighbor whom you know and trust or perhaps with friends who have babies of a similar age so that you can babysit for one another. Some areas have a babysitting cooperative whereby a group of people who know one another can babysit in exchange for points or tokens per hour. Going out together without the baby can help revive the feelings you shared before you had the baby and can cheer you up if either of you are feeling low.

If you are not working full-time, treat yourself to a few hours off now and again during the day. Leave the baby with a familiar person for two or three hours and do whatever you enjoy: go shopping, meet a friend for lunch, visit an art gallery.

Your health and looks are also important, so devote some time to them. Make sure that you eat well and that you are getting all the minerals and vitamins you need. You could have your hair cut in a new style, preferably one that looks good but needs minimum maintenance. Or treat yourself to some new clothes, possibly in different colors: a new look in hair or dress can be a great boost for a sagging morale.

Ten-minute ideas

When your baby has a nap or while your husband is amusing her, use the time for yourself. You would be amazed what you can achieve in only ten or fifteen minutes.

Try one of the following:
- ☐ Run a deep bath, put some foaming bath gel in it and enjoy a relaxing soak.
- ☐ Manicure and paint your fingernails – and/or your toenails.
- ☐ Give yourself a face massage, to leave your skin tingling. Massage your face, chin and neck, using cold cream or a special massage cream.
- ☐ Apply a fast-acting face pack for deep and thorough cleansing.
- ☐ Lie on the bed, or sit in a comfortable chair, to read a magazine, a chapter of your book, or the newspaper, in complete peace.
- ☐ Practice some deep breathing, or some relaxing yoga exercises.
- ☐ Telephone a friend for an uninterrupted chat.

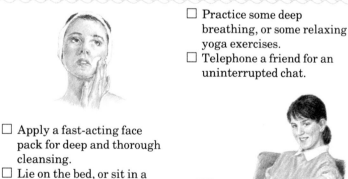

See Week 14 for Leaving Baby at Home

See Week 30 for Safety and the Mobile Baby

Week 39

Month: Dates:

MON

TUES

WED

THURS

FRI

SAT

SUN

Notes

COPYCAT

At this age your baby will probably start imitating gestures that you make, such as clapping hands and waving. He will probably find this very funny and may clap his hands or wave to get your attention. Help him to copy such gestures by playing games with him like "Peekaboo". Action rhymes like "Pat-a-cake" and "Pop goes the weasel" are also great fun at this stage.

The baby will also copy some of your gestures unconsciously, such as shaking his head to say "no" or drawing back and frowning when he sees something he doesn't like.

Don't forget that wooden spoons, cotton reels, cardboard boxes and tins to bang all make good toys. Your baby will love to have his own handbag and keys, too! If your baby is mobile, he will enjoy playing a simple game of "hide and seek" with you.

DON'T FORGET Write down when your baby gets her first tooth. The average baby gets her first tooth around seven to eight months.

Keeping baby amused

As your baby gets older, sleeps less and becomes more mobile you may find yourself trying to think of ways to amuse him. Babies soon become bored with the limited selection of toys available at home – rattles and soft toys are outgrown and first birthday presents are still some months away. If you are at home with your baby, you obviously can't expect him to amuse himself with toys all the time while you get on with housework. Try to create times every day when you play with your baby – if you meet his demands for attention then, he will be more likely to play by himself at other times.

Activities to enjoy together

There are lots of outside activities the enterprising mother can enjoy with her baby. Many older babies are not afraid of water and love their baths – this can be an ideal age to start taking them swimming. Some swimming pools have specially heated pools for younger children and regular sessions for mothers and babies, with water toys and equipment available. Babies who are prone to ear infections or chestiness, or who suffer from eczema, are better kept out of the pool for a little longer. Never immerse your baby totally in the pool, and try to prevent him drinking too much of the water.

Babies also enjoy visiting playgrounds designed for older children. Once a baby can sit up firmly he will enjoy a toddler swing which encloses him safely, especially if you say "boo" or tickle him when he swings close to you. Going with mother on a merry-go-round or slide can also be great fun.

Some local YWCA's organize special sessions for young children with trampolines, indoor slides and other equipment which a surprisingly young baby can enjoy. All these places are also good for meeting other mothers and children.

Action rhymes

"Pat-a-cake, pat-a-cake, baker's man
Bake me a cake as fast as you can
Prick it and pat it and mark it with "B"
And put it in the oven for baby and me."

Clap baby's hands in rhythm and imitate pricking and kneading.

"Clap hands, daddy comes
With his pockets full of plums."

Clap hands in rhythm and mime taking something out of pocket – describe large circle in the air for "plums".

"To market, to market, to buy a fat pig,
Home again, home again, jiggety jig
To market, to market, to buy a fat hog
Home again, home again, jiggety jog".

Put baby on your knee and jiggle him to the rhythm.

See Week 34 for Toys for the Older Baby

Visiting a playground

An outing to the local playground can be very exciting for your baby. Bear in mind that he may well be a little fearful the first time he goes on a slide or a swing. Hold him firmly and he will soon master his timidity and realize that such activities can be great fun.

Week 40

Month: _____   Dates: _____

MON

TUES

WED

THURS

FRI

SAT

SUN

Notes

STANDING

At around nine or ten months your baby may start pulling herself into the upright position using furniture or people as support. Her balance will, however, be very poor and she will easily fall over – she needs to cling on firmly with both hands.

Once your baby can pull herself up, she may have a problem because she is unable to sit down again. She will eventually learn to let go and sit down with a bump: you can help by giving her something soft to land on. She will lose confidence if she hurts herself.

If you support your baby under her arms, she will probably start to take steps and "walk" across the floor. Hold her very firmly because her balance is still precarious. Don't get trapped into spending hours walking up and down with your baby. It can be very tiring for you and won't help your baby walk unaided.

Weaning to a cup

When your baby is about nine months old you will probably want to start weaning her from breast or bottle for all but early morning or night feedings. If you have introduced a cup earlier, there should be no problem in offering a drink from a cup instead of a bottle at mealtimes or in between.

Many babies drink more than they actually need because sucking from a bottle gives them comfort. A baby who feeds from the breast for comfort often still gets a lot of her nourishment from breast-milk and may be reluctant to take other drinks or much solid food. So when you first offer the cup regularly you may find your baby drinks less than usual, but this is not a cause for concern: she will not let herself go thirsty for long.

Babies vary greatly in their need to suck for comfort, and some mothers will find that they can drop all breast- or bottle-feedings around the end of the first year. Some babies love their bedtime feeding, however, and are not ready to give it up at this stage; if you feel your baby shouldn't have a bottle after the age of one, then get her used to a cup early and cut down bottles gradually to help make weaning less of a struggle than leaving it till she is older.

Today there are excellent plastic spouted cups which the baby has to half-suck, half-drink, which makes weaning to a cup easier than it used to be. Some have handles, some not, and some are weighted at the bottom to help prevent them tipping over; in some the fluid comes out more quickly than others. Try out a few different kinds till you find which one your baby likes best.

You can give your baby milk or fruit juice in a cup, or water if your baby will drink it. If you give fruit juices, dilute these with three or four parts of water as undiluted fruit juice is very sweet or sometimes slightly acid and may not be very thirst-quenching either. Once your baby is used to undiluted juice it will be harder to get her to accept more dilute drinks.

Drinking from a cup is much less likely to damage your baby's teeth than drinking from a bottle, so this is a habit that is worth encouraging early.

Changing sleep patterns

Towards the end of the first year your baby's sleeping pattern may alter as she needs less sleep. A baby who had two good naps a day may wake after a shorter period or drop one nap altogether. Often the baby's morning nap will get later and later so that you are either giving her an early lunch and putting her to bed after it, or letting your baby sleep through her lunchtime and perhaps wake too early from her nap because she is hungry.

You can't make your baby sleep unless she is tired, so you may just have to accept that there will be times when her routine alters and be prepared to adjust. If you spend most of the morning trying one way or another to get your reluctant baby to sleep, you are both likely to end up cross and frustrated, with nothing at all achieved from your efforts.

If you time naps right, so that your baby is really tired before you put her down, she may go to sleep without any trouble, whereas twenty minutes earlier she would have made a fuss.

Even if she is not ready to sleep, put her in her crib with toys to play with. Let her grumble or cry for a short while – she may well settle down and amuse herself for some time even if she doesn't actually go to sleep.

See Week 23 for Using a Cup

See Week 50 for Weaning from Breast or Bottle

Week 41

Month: Dates:

MON

TUES

WED

THURS

FRI

SAT

SUN

Notes

ENCOURAGING SPEECH

The most important way in which you can help your baby to speak is to talk to him, sing to him and play verbal games with him. He needs this one-to-one contact to develop his speech and, above all, to teach him that talking is fun. Remember to name objects in everyday use and repeat them so that he learns their meaning. Ask him questions such as "Do you want a drink?" just before you pour him one.

At around nine months your baby will start to "take part" in adult discussions. He will follow a conversation between you and a friend, turning his head from one to the other as you speak. Often he will try to join in, laughing when you laugh, making loud exclamations or babbling away himself.

Babies vary greatly in the age at which they start to use real words, so don't be too anxious if you can't make out any words by the end of the first year. They understand a great deal of your speech before learning to talk themselves, so it's more important to check that he understands you and responds to your voice.

Communication

Although most babies don't produce their first intelligible word until at least their first birthday, preparation for speech starts a lot earlier. From as early as six weeks he will have been making cooing sounds and by around six months the familiar "babble" begins – long strings of sounds, like "ababa-ba" and "dadadada". At all these stages you can encourage your child to develop speech by talking back and responding. Let him enjoy the sounds he makes and help him to feel that he is communicating something.

Words and pictures
Looking at books together is a good way to introduce your baby to new words, other than those he hears every day. Name each picture for him, as you turn the pages, and he will soon try to repeat the sounds back to you.

A baby also needs to use his mouth in different ways to learn how to make sounds and develop the muscles that are needed to form noises. Too much sucking on pacifiers and bottles can deter the baby from developing these muscles; breast-feeding on the other hand will have given him a good start as it develops strong muscles in the mouth and jaw. Babies should also get used to biting and chewing food and getting their tongues around different textures.

Somewhere around nine or ten months babies learn to get what they want by pointing. This is a big step in learning to communicate and also in developing language, since when the baby points the mother can give the object a name. He may come to understand several words even if he is unable to speak them and will find a way of clearly showing that he understands; if you say "clap" he may clap his hands and when you say, "bye bye", wave his hand.

Baby language
At about nine months a baby's babble becomes more complicated as different sounds creep in. He may make more complicated sounds like "mum" and "shhh" and will also invent little words like "mabu" and "updi" which may mean little to anybody else.

Your baby may sometimes sound as if he is actually talking, but in a foreign language! Interestingly, the babble of children from different countries appears to be broadly similar, and is little influenced by the language the baby hears. Similarly, deaf children often babble quite normally and speech problems occur only later.

You may find it difficult to distinguish your baby's first words because they are not clear and are only approximations of the real word. However, a baby is using a "word" if he uses the same sound to indicate the same object. He may, for example, say "da" when he wants a drink from his cup, or "tu" for shoe. A great deal of confusion exists as to whether, when he says "dada" or "mama", he really means daddy and mommy. Sometimes he does, but these are sounds used frequently and often not for any particular reason. And because it is easier to say, "dada" often comes before "mama" much to many mothers' disgust!

See
Week 50 for
First Words

Week 42

Month: Dates:

MON

TUES

WED

THURS

FRI

SAT

SUN

Notes

VACATION EQUIPMENT

☐ Pack a travel bag with your baby's things and keep it handy on the journey (see Week 31, What to Take on a Vacation).

☐ Take a light, folding stroller if you are traveling with a loaded car or by train or plane.

☐ You may need a comfortable sling or backpack if you are going to do any walking.

☐ You can get portable child seats in several forms – some versions clip or screw on to the side of a table, booster seats fit on top of a chair, and there are cloth traveling seats which fit over the back of a chair and keep baby secure.

☐ A portacrib will be essential if a crib is not provided. Where a crib *is* provided, check that it has the safety features described in Week 11, Choosing a Crib.

A portable child seat which clamps to a table can be a real boon in hotels, restaurants or while visiting friends, making all the difference to an enjoyable meal out.

Family vacations

At some point in your baby's first year you are likely to go away on a vacation as a family. It is worth giving a lot of thought as to what kind of vacation will be best; accept that you might want a very different kind of vacation from the type you had as a couple.

If you want to go out in the evenings, you will have to go somewhere where babysitting is available or take a friend, relative or nanny along with you. If you go to a hotel, you will need to check whether they have facilities for babies and perhaps a babysitting service, so that you can eat your evening meal without worrying whether the baby will wake and cry. You may also want to know if they cater to children in other ways, perhaps preparing special food or having equipment you might want, like highchairs in the dining room and a crib and bedding so you don't have to take you own – or a children's pool.

Young children often react badly to heat, so beware of going anywhere very hot. Babies easily develop rashes like prickly heat and their delicate skin also burns readily in hot sun. A beach vacation may be ruined by your baby's inability to sleep on hot nights – especially if you are all in a small room together and have neighbors banging on the walls at 2 a.m.! Some babies react to a change in the water with an upset stomach, so take something with you to boil water thoroughly. If your baby is bottle-fed, take the formula that she is used to.

Seaside vacations may seem ideal if you have a child, but in the first year your baby is unlikely to appreciate it all that much. Many babies will sit on the beach in the shade and play happily with a bucket and spade, at least for a while. But others eat the sand and pebbles on the beach and are afraid of the water. It is unlikely that you will be able to spend the whole day on the beach without her getting terribly bored.

Any vacation that involves you in much traveling, apart from getting there and back, is likely to be difficult – touring by car is unlikely to be very relaxing, and you may face problems in finding somewhere suitable to stay. But walking holidays can be successful if you have a comfortable backpack in which to carry the baby – most interesting walks will take you over paths where a stroller will be worse than useless.

Vacation choice

Hotel

√ If you pick the right hotel, you will have a real rest. There will be built-in babysitting and meals will be prepared for you.

✕ Possible problems with neighboring guests if your baby cries at night. Usually restricted room space.

Rental units with kitchens

√ Generally cheaper; easier to follow your home routine. Neighbors should be less of a problem.

✕ It may be difficult to find a babysitter if you want to go out. More work for you, especially if there is no washing machine.

Camping/Trailer

√ Some campsites or trailer sites are geared up with facilities for children. The baby will enjoy plenty of fresh air.

✕ More work for you – possible problems with neighbors if baby is noisy at night.

See Week 31 for Traveling with Baby

Week 43

Month: Dates:

MON

TUES

WED

THURS

FRI

SAT

SUN

Notes

FEEDING HIMSELF

Feeding himself is a big step towards baby's sense of independence and you should encourage it from an early stage, even if his first attempts are very clumsy and messy. If your baby feeds himself, he will take only as much as he needs and will not be tempted to overeat or, if you press food on him, reject food and become a difficult and fussy eater.

Give your baby a large, comfortable bib, put newspaper on the floor, give him a spoon – and let him get on with it. Use unbreakable bowls, preferably with a suction base, since these may end up on the floor. When he stops trying to eat and starts smearing food everywhere or throwing it on the floor, don't scold him – a little mess, after all, is good fun – but simply end the meal, clean him up and take him out of the highchair.

The older baby's diet

Your baby may now be eating a more or less adult diet, except that you should use no salt and reduce the sugar in cooking, and will need to mash or chop food appropriately. The textures your baby can cope with will depend partly on how many teeth are through; a late teether will find it much harder to manage raw apples, carrots and crusts than one whose teeth are through ahead of time. Some babies actively dislike lumpy food, but may prefer to help themselves to chopped pieces of food.

It will save you time if you adapt the food that you cook for yourselves for your baby, perhaps adding more salt or sugar after you have removed his portion. Steer clear of spices unless your baby is accustomed to them and avoid foods which are too rich, such as those with quantities of added cream and butter in them.

When buying ready-made food, check the ingredients carefully and try to avoid artificial colorings, flavorings and sweeteners, and check that they do not contain too much salt and sugar. Always buy the healthier version of a product: for example, choose brown rather than white rice, and ice cream made with cream, milk and eggs and with real fruit, rather than ice cream made from non-milk fat (often pork fat) with artificial colorings and flavorings, which is far less nutritious.

If you buy a lot of ready-made baby foods in boxes or jars do try to vary these as much as possible and make sure you buy foods appropriate for your baby's age. Buying food this way is likely to work out quite expensive but at least you will know the meals are well-balanced, should not contain harmful ingredients and have the necessary vitamins added. They are certainly much healthier than using convenience foods intended for adults which often have ingredients unsuitable for a young child.

Food additives – beware!

Today's foods contain several thousand chemical additives in the form of artificial colorings, flavorings, preservatives, and sweeteners. Fortunately, the majority of these additives are safe. But some additives in food are known to be linked to hyperactivity in sensitive children, and may be harmful in large quantities for all children. Those that have been linked with potential health hazards include several food colorings, sodium nitrate, sodium bisulfate, brominated vegetable oil, caffeine, BHT, MSG, and propyl gallate.

Reading labels can be confusing if you don't actually know what they mean. You can get hold of books which list the most common additives and information about them at your local library.

Many supermarket foods are now labeled as additive-free, but check these carefully; a can of baked beans advertised as low salt, no sugar and no artificial colorings or preservatives might contain large amounts of harmful saccharin instead of sugar, since saccharin is neither a coloring nor a preservative.

Below is a list of additives to try and avoid.
Blue 1 (Brilliant Blue FCF)
Blue 2 (Indigotine)
Citrus Red 2 – used by some Florida orange growers to cover up a green or yellow color on oranges, tangelos and temple oranges
Green 3 (Fast Green FCF)
Red 3 (Erthrosine)
Red 40 (Allura Red AC) – red, orange, brown or purple coloring
Yellow 5 (Tartrazine)
Yellow 6

The colors listed below are made from natural substances and have no known side-effects:
Riboflavin (vitamin B2) – yellow
Carrot oil – yellow
Beta-carotine (provitamin A) – yellow
Dehydrated beets – dark red
Annotto extract – yellowish red
Grape color extract – purple red

See Week 33 for Feeding the Older Baby

Week 44

Month: Dates:

MON

TUES

WED

THURS

FRI

SAT

SUN

Notes

◼ LOSING AND FINDING

At around this age a baby will be interested in letting go and looking for lost objects. She realizes that just because something has disappeared from her vision doesn't mean it's no longer there. She will drop things from her highchair and then bend over the edge to see where they have gone. If you hide an object under a bowl, box or cushion, she will know it is underneath and will enjoy removing whatever is concealing it to see the hidden object reappear.

You can make up many games which play on your baby's new discovery, such as hiding different objects under stacking cups, and playing "Which hand is it in?" She will love to try and open your hand to see what it's holding.

Your baby will be thrilled if you join in hide-and-seek games with her, hiding behind doors, under cushions or behind the sofa. It is amusing to see that the baby's idea of hiding is simply to conceal her head and not the rest of her body.

You can play games like this with your baby at the same time as you do the housework if you turn running into the kitchen or up the stairs into a game. Your baby will never tire of this game because it reassures her that while mommy has disappeared for a few moments, she will always come back again.

The frustrated baby

At around this age your baby – and you as parents – may discover that she has a will of her own, when she realizes that she is not able or allowed to do many of the things that she would like to do. Once she becomes mobile she may wish to explore every room of the house and open and shut every cupboard and container, remove the contents of every drawer and take to pieces anything that comes apart. You will need to create an environment that is safe and which at the same time frustrates her as little as possible.

Fortunately a baby of this age is easily distracted and you will quickly be able to switch her attention from the forbidden object to something else. However, it will have to be something interesting; the boring rattle she has already discarded just won't be an acceptable substitute. Taking the baby to another room or playing a game which commands her attention can make her forget something that she wanted to do. Some temptations will simply have to be removed or made safe, however, to prevent her heading for them every time they catch her eye.

Saying "no"

Despite all your safety precautions, there will be times when you will have to say "no", and at this age you can begin to teach your baby the meaning of this word. For some time she will have sensed approval or disapproval in your voice and you can use your voice to reinforce the message as you remove either her or the object which is forbidden. However, not all babies react in the same way; some treat "no" as a challenging game and repeat what they have been told not to do; others burst into tears at the first sign of disapproval. You can't expect a baby of this age to respond to a spoken command – you can only use it to back up your actions. If she learns by experience that she is not allowed to empty the contents of the refrigerator, she will eventually give up trying.

Physical limitations

If your baby wants to crawl but hasn't quite got the hang of it, or if she has mastered standing up but hasn't worked out how to sit down again without falling over, she is clearly going to be very frustrated with the limitations of her own body.

Try to make other things as easy as possible for her so she doesn't have too many frustrations to deal with. Find ways of helping her to achieve things she wants to do; for example, allow her to feed herself or help to transport her to where she wants to go, to give her a feeling of achievement and self-confidence. However, never try to force your baby to crawl or stand up if she isn't able to do it. If she tries to do these things before she's ready she could hurt herself and this will only add to her frustration.

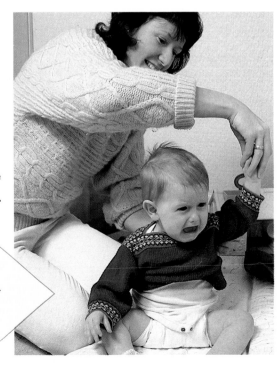

Showing resistance

A frustrated baby may resent being dressed or having her diaper changed and will resist with all her might, stiffening her limbs and making your job as difficult as possible! Try to remain patient.

See Week 30 for Safety and the Mobile Baby

Week 45

Month: Dates:

MON

TUES

WED

THURS

FRI

SAT

SUN

Notes

■ "CRUISING"

Once your baby has learned to pull himself up to a standing position it won't be long until he starts walking, using his hands to support him. This is known as cruising. At first he will progress slowly, and will need to hold on to something stable, like the bars of his playpen, the leg of a table or the back of a chair which will give him a good grip.

Next, he will take more weight on his feet and use his hands more for balance than actually to help support him. He will let go with one hand and move it to another support, or even use only one hand to balance with, perhaps holding a toy in the free hand. At this stage he will only let go of one support when he is confident that he has taken firm hold of another.

Later, your baby will be able to cruise along flat surfaces such as walls and will move from one piece of furniture to another, perhaps taking a brief step in between, so that he can gradually move all round a room without actually walking.

When your baby is learning to walk, it is best for him to go barefoot, as socks can make his feet slip and shoes are too constricting.

Toys to grow with

Unless Christmas falls at around this time in your baby's life, you may find you have a sudden dearth of suitable toys as he will have out grown those bought for the small baby. At this stage it might be worth investing in a few well-chosen toys which will last.

Shape-sorters and nesting boxes are reliable favorites; your baby will enjoy looking at different shapes and putting them in and out of the box well before he can use the appropriate holes. Toys where rings or other shapes are threaded on a central pole will interest a baby in different ways as his skills develop, and building blocks and simple construction toys may keep him amused for long periods, even if he can only take them apart at this stage. Some babies enjoy simple jigsaws where they can remove the pieces with little knobs. You will have to join in with this play; you put the toy back together, and the baby takes it apart.

Toys made from household objects will also keep your baby happy: boxes to crawl in and out of, cartons which he can fill and empty with objects like corks and cotton reels. All babies love to empty their mother's handbag, so why not take an old bag and fill it with things he can remove at will?

A baby of this age will enjoy a baby wagon which he can load with toys. Now is the time he will really need it, when he is learning to stand and walk, rather than waiting until his first birthday when he may be walking or be on the point of walking alone. Some push-along toys will convert later into cars to sit on and move around, or will have some other function, so these are worth considering. Before your baby starts using such toys, check that stairs are guarded and replace glass doors with safety glass.

Toys on strings are good at this age: your baby can pull them towards him as he sits and, when he learns to walk, pull them along behind him. Besides the simple wooden or plastic ones, there are also more interesting animals which wag their tails, shake their heads or make a noise as they are pulled along. Your baby may also be amused by puppets or dolls which you can operate for him.

Other favorite toys are a jack in the box (although these make some babies cry) and musical boxes which they can operate themselves by pulling a string or opening a lid. Many babies love anything musical and you can buy simple instruments, such as bells.

Books are popular with all young children, especially colorful picture books with bold images and little writing. From rag books and board books he can progress on to sturdy "real" books. You will need to turn the pages for him and name the pictures.

Buy a baby wagon that is heavy enough not to tip up when your baby puts his weight on it. He will get enjoyment from pushing it along until well into his second year.

See
Week 51
for Walking

See
Week 52
for First
Birthday
Presents

Week 46

Month: Dates:

MON

TUES

WED

THURS

FRI

SAT

SUN

Notes

■ EMERGENCY PROCEDURES

Burns and scalds
☐ Immerse the burned or scalded area in cold water for at least ten minutes.
☐ Take off any tight clothes.
☐ Call the doctor or go straight to the hospital.
☐ If a child's clothes are on fire, douse them with water or smother them with a towel, blanket or coat. As a last resort, use your own clothes and body to smother the flames. (Beware of using synthetic fabrics which could catch fire.)

Choking
☐ Hold your baby face down over your arm (or hold her by the legs and turn her upside down) and give her four sharp taps between the shoulder blades.
☐ If this doesn't work, sit her in front of you and, using two fingers of each hand, give four sharp thrusts to the upper abdomen (between the navel and the breastbone). This should make the child breathe out and dislodge the object.
☐ Never try to scoop out an object wedged at the back of her throat, as this could lodge it more firmly.

Poisoning
☐ If you think your baby has swallowed something poisonous, take her straight to the hospital, with the container if you know what it was.
☐ If she has swallowed something you have the slightest doubt about call the nearest poison control center.
☐ Keep syrup of Ipecac on hand in case the poison control center recommends it.

Electric shock
☐ Switch off the source of power or break the electrical contact: use something that won't transmit electricity (like a wooden broom) to push the baby away.

Safety and first aid

By the time your baby becomes upright and is very mobile you will have had to adapt your house to minimize the chances of an accident. If you are aware of the most common causes of accidents to children, you can do everything possible to avoid these. However, no matter how careful you are, there is always the possibility of an unforeseen happening and it is also important to know how to deal with an emergency if it arises. In rare instances you need to know how to do mouth-to-mouth resuscitation if the baby has stopped breathing, or heart compressions if her heart has stopped. You can best learn these by going on a first aid course such as those provided locally by organizations like The American Red Cross and your local first aid squad.

Burns and scalds are common serious accidents, so take sensible precautions to protect your child from these. Never put hot cups of tea and coffee within a baby's reach and always turn saucepan handles on the stove inwards. Make sure all fires are either guarded or put away; never leave electrical equipment plugged in.

Poisoning is another hazard, so keep all poisonous substances out of reach and locked up – not only medicines but also bleach, cleaning fluids and detergents. Where possible, buy these substances in bottles with child-resistant closures. Keep plastic bags out of baby's reach or punch holes in them.

Don't let your baby get hold of small objects which she could swallow and choke on. Ballpoint pen tops and the plastic clips used to fasten bags of bread are particularly dangerous items which have caused child deaths. Sharp pins and hooks are also potentially dangerous. Never leave your child unattended in the bath as a baby can drown in only a small depth of water.

Your child will have many falls and tumbles in her first year; she will usually howl when hurt and may develop bruises but most of the time it is unlikely to be serious.

Danger signals

If your baby bangs her head, take her to the doctor if she shows any of the following signs:
- ☐ She is unconscious, even briefly;
- ☐ She does not cry when hurt and is drowsy;
- ☐ She vomits after the accident;
- ☐ She is bleeding from the ears or nose;
- ☐ She is bleeding profusely;
- ☐ Her behavior appears abnormal to you.

Week 47

Month: _____ Dates: _____

MON

TUES

WED

THURS

FRI

SAT

SUN

Notes

FIRST AID KIT

It is useful to keep a first aid kit in the house and another in the car if you have one. Always remember to take one with you when you are on vacation and keep it in a safe place. You can buy ready-made first aid kits from the pharmacy, or you can make your own by getting a sturdy plastic box or tin and putting in essentials yourself. You will need adhesive bandages, gauze bandages, absorbent cotton, safety pins or surgical tape, blunt-ended tweezers, antiseptic cream or lotion, an antiseptic solution or surgical spirit (or antiseptic wipes for convenience), calamine lotion or soothing ointment for sunburn or stings, acetaminophen syrup, and a thermometer or "fever strip".

If your baby has more than a mild injury, you will need to use first-aid treatment or see a doctor (see Week 46). You can treat minor cuts and scrapes by cleaning the wound with warm water, applying antiseptic cream and covering with a bandage or dressing. Blisters should never be popped, and are best left alone; if a blister is somewhere where it is rubbing, cover it with a bandage or dressing. If the blister bursts, keep it clean and dry.

Small objects like a speck of dirt in the eye can usually be removed by bathing the eye with absorbent cotton and warm (preferably boiled) water. Don't let your child touch it. If the object is larger or won't come out, it is best to consult a doctor.

Many small children put foreign bodies in their ears or nose. Don't try to remove an object from the ear yourself as you may wedge it in more firmly – see a doctor instead. If there is a foreign body in the nose, block one nostril and get the child to blow through the other (this is difficult with a baby). If it won't come out, again see a doctor.

Small children can easily swallow a small, round object like a marble. Usually this will go through their system without causing any harm, but any signs of pain or discomfort should be taken seriously.

The older baby's clothes

As your baby gets older you will probably want to dress him or her in more individualistic clothes, but these should always be comfortable and practical. Dresses are pretty for little girls and are practical for the baby who sits or who is walking, but they are a nuisance for the crawler, who will constantly be kneeling on the hem and falling over it. If your baby girl does wear dresses, she will need warm tights to cover her diaper and keep her legs warm in winter, or bodysuits which fasten underneath to keep her stomach warm.

You can make clothes last a lot longer by buying sizes that are slightly too big for your baby. Larger clothes, being baggy, can be very comfortable, and by shortening straps and rolling up sleeves and trouser legs, you may find the clothes will fit your baby reasonably well now and will still be in use up to a year or more later.

First shoes

Do not be tempted to buy your baby's first shoes too early. It is usually best to wait until he is actually walking and you want him to walk around out of doors. His feet are growing very rapidly and may change shape when he starts walking properly, as they become more arched; they may also get wider as he puts his weight on them and the toes splay out. So shoes fitted before he is walking may not fit correctly, or may be outgrown, once he starts to walk.

Always take your baby to a proper shoe store to have his feet measured for his first shoes. You may find it best to invest in a good-quality leather shoe, especially for the first pair, since they will fit more comfortably and this may be important in giving your child confidence in walking.

Don't be tempted to buy shoes which are too big, for your child to grow into, as they will be uncomfortable and he may be always tripping over his toes. Check the baby's foot size frequently once he starts wearing shoes, as tight shoes will restrict growth and may even deform the foot.

Jogging suits and overalls are practical and popular for children of both sexes and are likely to last longer than all-in-one suits. Tight clothes will restrict your active baby's movements and you should never put on suits in which the toes are too tight, or socks that are too small, as this will restrict his growing feet. The feet of stretch suits and socks are slippery for a baby who is crawling, standing or learning to walk, so it is best for a mobile baby to go barefoot or, in winter, to wear soft corduroy footwear with non-slip soles which keep feet warm without restricting them. You can buy these practical shoe substitutes in various sizes; some have cords which you can tighten round the ankles and others have elastic. Check that there is plenty of room inside and that the elastic isn't too tight around the ankles. They are also very useful for outdoor wear in the winter if your baby's snow suit doesn't have toes (but not for outdoor walking).

For the winter, warm jackets and all-in-one suits are essential, and in really cold weather it is a good idea to have a hat that covers the ears or has ear-flaps. Keep something warm on the baby's feet in winter too. If you use mittens, try tying them together with string and threading them through the arms of his coat because he will probably try to pull them off all the time.

Week 48

Month: Dates:

MON

TUES

WED

THURS

FRI

SAT

SUN

Notes

◼ HEALTHY TEETH

Once your baby has several teeth, you can start to clean them after meals with a toothbrush and a small quantity of toothpaste. If you are giving fluoride supplements, beware of her swallowing much fluoride toothpaste or she may get too high a dose.

Never let your baby go to sleep sucking a bottle of milk or juice as this can damage her teeth, as well as possibly cause ear infections or allow her to choke.

Your baby's diet is also important for keeping teeth healthy. Cut out over-sweetened foods, especially in convenience meals, and don't give sweet things in between. If your baby wants a snack, try an unsweetened biscuit or cracker, lump of cheese or a piece of fruit.

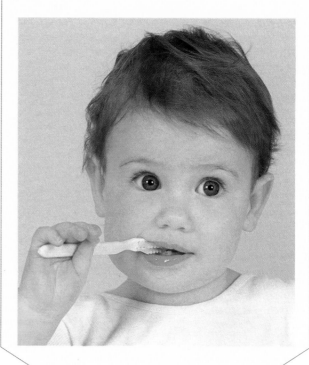

Caring for your older baby

As your baby gets older you might face problems in keeping her clean and well-cared for because she may resist all your attempts to do so. It can be a struggle to hold a wriggling baby down while you change her diaper; she may pull away and howl when you wipe her sticky face and hands; and she may refuse to keep still while you trim her nails and comb or cut her hair. The best way is to try to make a game out of all these activities and to choose your moment so as to get least resistance.

To make diaper changing easier, keep some interesting objects to entertain your baby while she's on the changing mat; give her them to look at before you lie her down rather than afterwards, when she's furious and howling and will probably just throw them away. Get everything ready before you change her so you don't have to fumble around looking for cream or pins, and lift her up as soon as the diaper is on, fastening clothing and tidying up when she's upright so she accepts that diaper changing is over in a few moments.

If she hates having her face and hands wiped, try using a warm soft cloth and tickle her with it a few times before giving her a gentle wipe. Play "This little piggy" with her fingers as you wipe them. You can try the same technique when cutting finger- and toenails: it helps if you cut these when she's out of a warm bath, when her nails are softer. Never force her to keep still, which can turn this exercise into a battle and make her resist further. If it's really impossible to get her cooperation, try to cut your baby's nails when she is fast asleep.

Some babies develop a dislike of having their hair washed when they get older. One trick is to wet the hair gently while she's in the bath, using as little water as possible, and shampoo it with the minimum of non-stinging shampoo. If the water temperature is just right, she will hardly notice it. Then take a towel or dry wash cloth and hold it over her forehead while you swiftly rinse the hair to prevent any water and shampoo from getting on her face and in her eyes. Again, turn swooshing the water down her back into a game and make her laugh. Then dry the hair quickly with a towel. If all else fails, you can buy a shampoo shield which helps to stop the water getting on to the child's face and into her eyes.

Your older baby will probably not mind being dressed and undressed too much and should be able to cooperate by moving her arms to get them in and out of armholes, rather than holding them poker-stiff. It helps to choose your moment tactfully and not swoop your baby up to dress or change her when she's absorbed in play or doing something interesting.

☐ To cut your baby's finger-nails, hold her hand gently but firmly and do let go if she resists. Try to make it into a game.

☐ Tickle your baby with a cloth or sponge before wiping her face and hands. Have the sponge warm and not too wet.

☐ You can get special shields to protect your baby's face while washing her hair, which can make for happier bathtimes.

Week 49

MON

TUES

WED

THURS

FRI

SAT

SUN

Notes

■ MESSY PLAY

Most babies love an opportunity to make a mess, though they're seldom allowed this luxury. If your baby seems bored or if you want to give him something new and exciting to do, why not set aside some time for this?

Put him in a highchair with a protective garment on and give him some paper and some finger-paints. If you think he can wield a brush, you could give him a brush and some trays of paint. Use an egg carton or other box to put paint in; if you put a piece of sponge in the bottom to soak up most of the paint, you will avoid spills. He may also enjoy "drawing" a picture with stubby wax crayons; you could sit him on your lap for this more controllable activity.

Make up some "play dough" with flour and water and let him poke, knead and finger it to his heart's content. Again, restrain him in the highchair if you don't want it to end up all over the room. In the summer, let him play with sand and water outdoors.

A baby's attention span is very short at this age and he may be interested in one of these activities for only two or three minutes. This will seem a short time for all the preparation and mess involved, but he will gradually want to play for longer and longer periods.

Meeting other children

Young babies do not on the whole pay much attention to other babies of the same age — they may smile at them as they would at other friendly faces but they are unlikely to interact much. By the time they are sitting, they may try to grab at and "explore" each other, take hold of each other's toys or pull clothes and hair. They will not really "play" together till the age of eighteen months or more, and then quite a lot of their interaction will consist of fighting over toys.

Nevertheless, it's a good thing for your baby to get used to being with other children in preparation for later on, when children really need to socialize. It's important to teach your child to share, not just toys and games but also your attention. Minding a friend's baby for a morning on an exchange basis can teach him that he can't always have your individual attention. And although two babies may seem not to interact, you may notice that they play quietly together on the floor for longer than they would normally do on their own. Babies of this age will sometimes imitate each other's gestures, such as clapping hands and waving, and will find this very amusing.

You can also take your baby to local parks and playgrounds and other similar places where there are small children. He may enjoy the noise and activity even if he is too young to join in with many of the activities. With more and more children being reared today in homes where they are the only children around, the importance of playgroups and nursery schools has never been greater. Most experts agree that it is vital for children to have many opportunities for interacting with children their own age and learning social skills before starting school.

It is a good idea to join a local mother and toddler group, especially if you don't know many mothers in the area with children of the same age as yours. If there aren't any in your area, the end of your baby's first year might be a good time to get together with some other local mothers to organize a local playgroup for when the children are ready. The National Association for the Education of Young Children can provide information on how to set up a playgroup (see Useful Addresses p.110).

Setting up a playgroup

You can run a playgroup either in a communal space like a church or village hall or, if this isn't available, on a rotating basis in your own houses. It might be a good idea to contact the local governing body or church to find out if there are any funds for setting up a playgroup and buying equipment.

You will need to insure yourselves and to buy some basic equipment, including large items not available for the children at home. You may be able to buy equipment second-hand or borrow from other local groups.

Shared outings
An outing to the park on a sunny day takes on a new dimension when sharing the experience with another mother. Other mothers are the perfect audience for airing your worries or discussing your baby's progress, because they are as interested in small children as you are! It is surprising how much quite young children will also enjoy each other's company, even when there is some difference in their ages.

Week 50

Month: _____   Dates: _____

MON

TUES

WED

THURS

FRI

SAT

SUN

Notes

FIRST WORDS

Your baby may produce her first words at around this time. Even if she doesn't produce anything intelligible, she will carry out long conversations with you in quite complex babble, some of which may carry the same inflexions as adult speech. If you sing to her, you may find that she sings along too in a reasonably good approximation of the tune.

It's very important to talk to your baby at this stage. She will take great pleasure in your imitating the sounds she makes and in trying to copy the sounds you make. She will also understand a great deal of what you say and you can play simple "Where is it?" games together. Ask: "Where's mommy's nose?" and point to that. Your baby will soon catch on and may do the pointing herself.

Weaning from breast or bottle

By the end of the first year, your baby will probably be ready to give up breast- or bottle-feedings entirely. Whether you decide to wean her from the breast or put away the bottle at this stage depends partly on you and partly on the baby. Some mothers find that their baby gradually loses interest, so that when you sit down to breast-feed her she laughs, giggles, tries to stand up or wriggle off your lap. She may start to feed and then, perhaps when your milk lets down, lose interest and do something else.

A bottle-fed baby may drink less and less of her bottle, or resent having to sit still on your lap while she takes it. A baby who behaves like this is really trying to tell you that she's ready to give up, and will not miss the breast- or bottle-feedings if you stop them.

If you are ready to wean your baby from the breast or don't want her to continue having a bottle, you will probably jump at this opportunity. But some mothers enjoy breast-feeding so much that they don't want to stop yet, and others are convinced that without their bedtime bottle-feeding their baby won't go to sleep.

Some babies, on the other hand, really seem to need to suck for longer and will be happier continuing with a bedtime breast- or bottle-feeding. If your baby wants to suck but you feel it is time to wean her from the breast, you might be advised to give a bottle instead if she'll take it, although many babies will not.

Provided you never let a bottle-fed baby wander off with a bottle in her hand, she may not realize that she can do this and will be more willing to give up the bottle because there are other things she would rather do. A baby who learns that she can carry her bottle with her wherever she goes is less likely to give it up at the end of her first year.

Don't worry at this stage about your baby not drinking enough milk. Provided she is getting a good diet in other ways, milk is not essential, although it can be a useful source of protein and vitamins throughout childhood. If your baby still drinks a lot of milk, you may find she becomes more fussy about her meals because she is not really hungry. Overcome this problem by giving milk after a meal rather than before or with food.

Balanced meals for an older baby

Soups

You can make easy and nutritious soups for your baby and the whole family. Simply cook vegetables till soft, with chicken or other stock, and use a food mill or blender to liquidize it so that nothing is lost. Try old favorites like pea and ham (use dried split peas), and carrot and orange. You can add pasta shapes to the soup or break a whole egg into it shortly before serving.

Children often love to dip things in their food, so try making bread "animals". Thicken soup with yogurt or breadcrumbs.

Sandwiches

Sandwiches can provide a healthy balanced meal for your older baby. Choose wholewheat bread, butter thinly and use a variety of fillings – peanut butter (smooth, preferably without salt), cheese, boiled egg, minced roast chicken, beef or lamb, and tomatoes, cucumber (chopped) or fruit such as bananas or ripe pears. Use a pie cutter to make interesting shapes.

Try to use bread which is not too dry or crumbly, and cut off the crusts if your baby always leaves them. Avoid "granary" style bread.

Alternative ideas

If your child dislikes certain foods, you can usually find alternatives she prefers. A baby who doesn't like vegetables can get most of the vitamins and fiber from fruit instead; a baby who doesn't like meat can get protein from dairy products, fish (try mild-tasting, soft fish like flounder or cod) and eggs. Or you can try some health food products such as tofu (soya bean spread), which is very bland in taste and texture and can easily be mixed in with other foods, or seed spreads like tahini.

See
Week 40
for Weaning
to a Cup

Week 51

Month: *Dates:*

MON

TUES

WED

THURS

FRI

SAT

SUN

Notes

▪ WALKING

The majority of babies do not actually walk till after their first birthday – the average age is about thirteen months. However, your baby will probably now be on the threshold of walking, and some children take their first steps a few weeks before they actually learn to walk alone.

You can encourage your child to take a few steps by crouching down in front of him, holding out your arms and catching him when he launches himself forward. Once he has taken a step or two, move slowly a little further away. He will probably fall over a lot when he is first walking, so don't let him walk on very hard or rough surfaces where he could hurt himself and lose confidence.

Your baby will be encouraged to take his first few steps if you hold out your hands to him.

Your baby's first few unsupported steps will be a moment you will never forget.

You: one year later

A whole year has passed since your baby was born. You may find it hard to believe how quickly the time has gone and how much you have changed in the meantime. Your life is now probably very different in many ways from how it was before you were a mother and now is a good time to take stock. You may find being a full-time mother very rewarding and have made lots of friends with whom to share the experience. On the other hand, you may be finding that

Another baby?
Some mothers feel that now is the time to plan a second baby so that the two children are close in age. Others feel they cannot contemplate another child for some time yet.

after a year dedicated to the baby you want to do more for yourself and perhaps take on some part-time work or a daytime or evening adult education class to develop other aspects of yourself. You may want to spend more time with your partner and create some time for the two of you to be alone.

A year after the birth you may be thinking about when is the best time to plan another baby – unless you have decided that one is enough! Mothers often wonder if there is a "best" gap between two children in a family. The answer is probably not; there are advantages and disadvantages to each age gap. Any gap under eighteen months is likely to be physically very hard on the mother but would enable her to go back to work once her family is complete, without being at home for too many years. A short age gap is also very hard for the elder child, who will still really be a baby himself when the second baby arrives.

A short gap may mean that there is almost no break between the end of breast-feeding and the start of another pregnancy, so the drain on your body is considerable. A close gap also means two babies in diapers at the same time, that you may be dealing with toilet training as well as constantly feeding a small baby, and that you may

frequently have to carry both baby and toddler up and down stairs. On the other hand, the elder child may be too young to express much jealousy and will soon adjust to the new baby because he can't remember that life was any different. When the children grow older they will be closer developmentally and may play very well together for that reason.

A larger gap is likely to be less exhausting for the mother; there will be a period in which to recover from the first baby before entering the second pregnancy and perhaps a break from diapers and broken nights as well. If the elder child is at nursery school there will be more time for you to give to each child individually. However, older children may be more jealous of a baby as they can understand more what is going on and can remember what life was like before they had to share their parents' love. Later on, if their interests and skills are very different, they may be less good playmates. However, the second child often acquires skills at an earlier age, especially if helped by an older brother or sister, and the two can have great fun together.

See Week 47 for First Shoes

Week 52

Month: _____   Dates: _____

MON

TUES

WED

THURS

FRI

SAT

SUN

Notes

■ FIRST BIRTHDAY PRESENTS

Friends and relatives will probably buy presents for your baby and may well consult you on what she would like. Give some thought to this, as you may already have bought some obvious toys and may prefer toys that your baby will grow into around eighteen months.

A ride-on toy, such as a simple tricycle (without pedals) or a car which the child propels with her legs, will start to be fun soon after the age of one. She will get a lot of pleasure from a traditional jointed teddy bear now so this is a good idea for a present, provided she was not given one at birth. From around twelve months children start to get real enjoyment out of books. Pop-up books and activity books of different kinds provide novel entertainment, and she will continue to love picture books with bold illustrations.

A blackboard and easel will come in at some time during the second year, and can be adapted for a variety of different uses. Toddlers also love a play house. For the summer months, a paddling pool or sandpit makes good outdoor play equipment.

■ **DON'T FORGET** Your baby will need a measles mumps and rubella (MMR) vaccination around the age of fifteen months.

First birthday

Your baby's first birthday is a very special occasion and it is worth giving some thought to how you would like to celebrate it. Your baby is unlikely to know what is going on herself, so plan how you think she would like to spend the day, and decide what you and your partner can do to make it special. It need not cost very much.

Other babies of this age are unlikely to interact much so a children's party, as such, is not really appropriate. However, you could ask other mothers and babies over and make some sandwiches and a special cake – perhaps something simple and nutritious like the carrot cake recipe (right). You can decorate the cake with fruit or other edible decorations to make it attractive and colorful for your baby's enjoyment.

You may decide that a family get-together is the most suitable form of celebration, with you and grandparents and perhaps other close family members or friends whom your baby knows well.

You may like to spend a quiet evening with your partner thinking about the events of a year ago and looking at photographs, recalling details of the birth and how you felt about it. In the everyday hurly-burly of looking after your child, it is easy to lose sight of how miraculous her birth was.

Party carrot cake
8oz flour (wholewheat if preferred)
2 tsp baking powder
4oz finely grated carrot
4oz butter
4oz brown sugar
grated rind of a lemon or orange
2 eggs, lightly beaten
1 fl oz milk
Cream together butter and sugar, then add rind and eggs and beat till smooth. Add carrot, then gradually add flour and baking powder and use milk if required to make a soft mixture.

Grease a cake tin and fill it with the mixture. Bake in a preheated oven (325°F) for 45–60 minutes, or until the cake is well-risen and golden brown.

Cheese and fruit topping:
6oz cream cheese
3oz fruit purée
Mix the cream cheese and fruit purée together and use to fill the cake and cover the top. Decorate with pieces of fruit. You can make a face or picture on the cake with fruit or other decorations.

Helping your baby enjoy her birthday
☐ Babies love tearing wrappers off presents, so don't tie things up so well that she is frustrated. Remove the sticky tape to give her a helping hand before she unwraps it herself.
☐ Try hiding presents around the house so that she comes across them unexpectedly. A present will seem doubly interesting if she's found it for herself.
☐ You could try wrapping up a cracker or an apple in wrapping paper for her at snack times, or even her drinking cup or bottle.
☐ Blow up some balloons and scatter them around the house – babies love to play with them until they go pop.
☐ Don't get so involved in preparations for a party that you don't manage to give the baby enough of your attention – which she will value far more.

See Week 45 for Toys to Grow With

Useful addresses

POSTNATAL SUPPORT

La Leche League International
9616 Minneapolis Ave.
Franklin Park, IL 60131
312-455-7730
Breastfeeding information and
support. (Check phone directory for
local chapter or write to the above
address.)

**National Sudden Infant Death
Syndrome Foundation**
822 Professional Place,
Suite 104 Landover, MD 20785
301-459-3388
800-221-SIDS (toll-free)
Referrals to local chapters.

Parent Care
101½ S. Union St.
Alexandria, VA 22314
703-836-4678
Information and support for parents
of premature and high-risk infants.

**National Organization of
Mothers of Twins Clubs Inc.**
12404 Princess Jeanne NE
Albuquerque, NM 87112-4640
505-275-0955

**Postpartum Support
International**
c/o Jane Honikman
927 N. Kellogg Ave.
Santa Barbara, CA 93111
805-967-7636
Self-help mutal aid group to support
mothers with postpartum emotional
syndrome.

SUPPORT AND INFORMATION FOR PARENTS

Children in Hospitals
31 Wilshire Park
Needham, MA 02192
508-369-4467
Offers help and advice on
negotiating with hospital staff in
order to minimize the trauma of
hospitalization.

**American Association For
Marriage and Family Therapy**
1717 K St. N.W., Suite 407
Washington, DC 20006
202-429-1825
Provides lists of division presidents
in your area.

Childhelp U.S.A.
P.O. Box 630
Hollywood, CA 90028
800-4-A-CHILD (24-hour hotline
for victims of child abuse, parents
who think they might abuse their
children, and anyone reporting
suspected child abuse.)

Parents Anonymous
6733 South Sepulveda Blvd.,
Suite 270
Los Angeles, CA 90045
Counseling for parents who have or
who are tempted to abuse their
children.
(Check phone directory for local
chapter or write to the above
address.)

**Mother's Center Development
Project**
336 Fulton Ave.
Hempstead, NY 11550
516-486-6614 (in NY state only)
800-645-3828 (toll-free outside NY
state)
Help in locating mothers' centers
near you and/or information on how
to start one.

**National Association for the
Education of Young Children**
1834 Connecticut Ave. N.W.
Washington, DC 20009
202-232-8777
800-232-8777 (toll-free)
Information about early child care
programs.

**March of Dimes Birth Defects
Foundation**
1275 Mamaroneck Ave.
White Plains, NY 10605
914-428-7100
800-626-2410 (toll-free)
Organizes support groups for
families of children with birth
defects.

United Way of America
701 N. Fairfax
Alexandria, VA 22314
703-836-7100
Several thousand United Way
offices throughout the country
provide information and referrals to
health and human care services.

**American Speech-Language-
Hearing Association**
10801 Rockville Pike
Rockville, MD 20852
301-897-8682
800-638-8255 (toll-free, voice and
TDD)
Information on communicative
disorders in children.

**Child Welfare League of
America – Research Center**
440 1st St. N.W., Suite 310
Washington, DC 20001
202-638-2952
Information on day care in centers
and homes.

INFORMATION ON HEALTH, SAFETY AND FIRST AID

**American Academy of
Pediatrics**
141 Northwest Point Blvd.
P.O. Box 927
Elk Grove Village, IL 60007
312-228-5005
800-421-0589 (toll-free IL only)
800-433-9016 (toll-free)
Information and referrals.

American Red Cross
National Headquarters
17th and D Sts. N.W.
Washington, DC 20006
202-737-8300

**National Highway Traffic Safety
Administration**
U.S. Department of Transportation
400 7th St., N.W.
Washington, DC 20590
202-366-0123
800-424-9393 (toll-free outside
Washington, DC for information
about car seats and automotive
safety).

National Safety Council
444 N. Michigan Ave.
Chicago, IL 60611
312-527-4800
800-621-7618 (toll-free)
or 800-621-7619 (toll-free)
Publishes material on safe toys and
furniture, safety restraints, etc.

**U.S. Consumer Product Safety
Commission**
1750 K St. N.W.
Washington, DC 20207
800-638-2772 (toll-free for
complaints about faulty items and
information on safe ones)

**National Center for Education in
Maternal and Child Health**
38th and R Sts. N.W.
Washington, DC 20057
202-625-8400
Information on maternal and child
health topics.

**Physicians for Automotive
Safety**
16 Hobart Gap Road
Short Hills, NJ 07078
800-624-0809 (toll-free)
Information about automotive
safety and baby care.

Index

Acknowledgments

Conran Octopus wish to thank the following for their help in the preparation of this book:

For her invaluable help with the American edition: Emily Van Ness

For advising on the text: Ros Meek, Assistant Public Relations Officer, Health Visitors' Association.

For design help: Claire Graham, David Warner

For taking part in the photography: Edward and Jeremy Hamand, Jill Embleton and Tom Peace, Henry Painter, Leonora Russell, Rona Skene

For jacket photographs: Andy Cox (front jacket); Guillaume de Laubier/Pix (back jacket)

For their permission to reproduce photographs: 1 Tim Woodcock; 2 Jennie Woodcock; 4 Loisjoy Thurston/Bubbles; 7 Jean-Pierre Crampion/Jerrican; 8 Anthea Sieveking/Vision International; 9 Sandra Lousada/Susan Griggs Agency; 14 Loisjoy Thurston/Bubbles; 16 Sally & Richard Greenhill; 18 Sandra Lousada/Susan Griggs Agency; 19 Chris Fairclough Colour Library; 29 Loisjoy Thurston/Bubbles; 23 Tony Stone Photo Library; 24 Guillaume de Laubier/Pix; 27 Pascal Hinous/Agence Top; 28 Valerie Clement/Jerrican; 37, 39 Sally & Richard Greenhill; 41 Pictor International; 42 Jennie Woodcock; 45 Pictor International; 47 Zefa Picture Library; 51 Jaqui Farrow/Bubbles; 54 Pictor International; 61 Zefa Picture Library; 67 Jeremy Hamand; 69 Sandra Lousada/Conran Octopus; 71 Lupe Cunha; 77 Jean François Besnard/Agence Top; 79 Sandra Lousada/Susan Griggs Agency; Loisjoy Thurston/Bubbles; 87 Jennie Woodcock; 89 François Lamy/Agence Top; 90 Loisjoy Thurston/Bubbles; 93 Lupe Cunha; 100, 103 Loisjoy Thurston/Bubbles; 104 Janine Wiedel; 107 Zefa Picture Library; 108 Nikki Gibbs/Bubbles.